Selected Poems
by Whitman

Selected Poems by Whitman

Walt Whitman

Thorndike Press • Waterville, Maine

Thorndike Press® Large Print Classics.

The tree indicium is a trademark of Thorndike Press.

The text of this Large Print edition is unabridged. Other aspects of the book may vary from the original edition.

Set in 16 pt. Plantin by Ramona Watson.

Printed in the United States on permanent paper.

Library of Congress Cataloging-in-Publication Data

Whitman, Walt, 1819–1892.
    [Poems. Selections]
    Selected poems by Whitman / by Walt Whitman.
       p. cm. — (Thorndike Press large print classics)
    Previously published: Poems / Whitman ; this selection by Peter Washington. New York : Knopf, c1994, in series: Everyman's library pocket poets.
    ISBN 0-7862-8604-0 (lg. print : hc : alk. paper)
    I. Washington, Peter. II. Title. III. Series.
PS3203.W37 2006
  811′.3—dc22   2006006051

Selected Poems
by Whitman

Contents

Birds of Passage 9
These Carols 9
Poets to Come 10
I Hear America Singing 11
Native Moments 12
When I Heard at the Close
    of the Day 13
Roots and Leaves Themselves Alone . . 15
I Saw in Louisiana a Live-Oak
    Growing 16
To a Stranger 17
A Glimpse 18
Among the Multitude 19
Youth, Day, Old Age and Night 20
A Noiseless Patient Spider 21
Me Imperturbe 22
My Picture-Gallery 23
A Hand-Mirror 24
Halcyon Days 25
The Dalliance of the Eagles 26
Old Salt Kossabone 27
A Twilight Song 29
The Runner 30
Perfections 30

O Tan-Faced Prairie-Boy 31
Sometimes with One I Love 31
Whoever You Are Holding Me
    Now in Hand 32
A Sight in Camp in the Daybreak
    Gray and Dim 35
Vigil Strange I Kept on the
    Field One Night. 37
An Army Corps on the March 39
Cavalry Crossing a Ford 40
The Wound-Dresser 41
Reconciliation 46
As I Lay with My Head in Your Lap
    Camerado 47
Crossing Brooklyn Ferry 48
There Was a Child Went Forth. 60
Starting from Paumanok 64
Song of Myself 86
The Sleepers. 193
Passage to India 212
Out of the Cradle Endlessly
    Rocking. 229
When Lilacs Last in the Dooryard
    Bloom'd 240
Whispers of Heavenly Death. 255
So Long! 256

BIRDS OF PASSAGE
Song of the Universal

I

Come said the Muse,
Sing me a song no poet yet has chanted,
Sing me the universal.

In this broad earth of ours,
Amid the measureless grossness and the
    slag,
Enclosed and safe within its central heart,
Nestles the seed perfection.

By every life a share or more or less,
None born but it is born, conceal'd or
    unconceal'd the seed is waiting.

1874

THESE CAROLS

These carols sung to cheer my passage
    through the world I see,
For completion I dedicate to the Invisible
    World.

1871

9

POETS TO COME

Poets to come! orators, singers, musicians
    to come!
Not to-day is to justify me and answer
    what I am for,
But you, a new brood, native, athletic,
    continental, greater than before
    known,
Arouse! for you must justify me.

I myself but write one or two indicative
    words for the future,
I but advance a moment only to wheel
    and hurry back in the darkness.

I am a man who, sauntering along
    without fully stopping, turns a casual
    look upon you and then averts his
    face,
Leaving it to you to prove and define it,
Expecting the main things from you.

1860

I HEAR AMERICA SINGING

I hear America singing, the varied carols
    I hear,
Those of mechanics, each one singing his
    as it should be blithe and strong,
The carpenter singing his as he measures
    his plank or beam,
The mason singing his as he makes ready
    for work, or leaves off work,
The boatman singing what belongs to
    him in his boat, the deck-hand
    singing on the steamboat deck,
The shoemaker singing as he sits on his
    bench, the hatter singing as he stands,
The wood-cutter's song, the ploughboy's
    on his way in the morning, or at
    noon intermission or at sundown,
The delicious singing of the mother, or of
    the young wife at work, or of the girl
    sewing or washing,
Each singing what belongs to him or her
    and to none else,
The day what belongs to the day — at
    night the party of young fellows,
    robust, friendly,
Singing with open mouths their strong
    melodious songs.

1860

NATIVE MOMENTS

Native moments — when you come upon
    me — ah you are here now,
Give me now libidinous joys only,
Give me the drench of my passions, give
    me life coarse and rank,
To-day I go consort with Nature's
    darlings, to-night too,
I am for those who believe in loose
    delights, I share the midnight orgies
    of young men,
I dance with the dancers and drink with
    the drinkers,
The echoes ring with our indecent calls,
    I pick out some low person for my
    dearest friend,
He shall be lawless, rude, illiterate, he
    shall be one condemn'd by others for
    deeds done,
I will play a part no longer, why should I
    exile myself from my companions?
O you shunn'd persons, I at least do not
    shun you,
I come forthwith in your midst, I will be
    your poet,
I will be more to you than to any of the
    rest.

1860

WHEN I HEARD AT THE CLOSE OF THE DAY

When I heard at the close of the day how
    my name had been receiv'd with
    plaudits in the capitol, still it was not
    a happy night for me that follow'd,
And else when I carous'd, or when my
    plans were accomplish'd, still I was
    not happy,
But the day when I rose at dawn from the
    bed of perfect health, refresh'd,
    singing, inhaling the ripe breath of
    autumn,
When I saw the full moon in the west
    grow pale and disappear in the
    morning light,
When I wander'd alone over the beach,
    and undressing bathed, laughing with
    the cool waters, and saw the sun rise,
And when I thought how my dear friend
    my lover was on his way coming,
      O then I was happy,
O then each breath tasted sweeter,
    and all that day my food nourish'd
    me more, and the beautiful day
    pass'd well,
And the next came with equal joy, and
    with the next at evening came my
    friend,

And that night while all was still I heard
    the waters roll slowly continually up
    the shores,
I heard the hissing rustle of the liquid
    and sands as directed to me
    whispering to congratulate me,
For the one I love most lay sleeping by
    me under the same cover in the cool
    night,
In the stillness in the autumn moonbeams
    his face was inclined toward me,
And his arm lay lightly around my breast
    — and that night I was happy.

                                    1860

ROOTS AND LEAVES THEMSELVES ALONE

Roots and leaves themselves alone are
    these,
Scents brought to men and women from
    the wild woods and pond-side,
Breast-sorrel and pinks of love, fingers
    that wind around tighter than vines,
Gushes from the throats of birds hid in
    the foliage of trees as the sun is risen,
Breezes of land and love set from living
    shores to you on the living sea, to
    you O sailors!
Frost-mellow'd berries and Third-month
    twigs offer'd fresh to young persons
    wandering out in the fields when the
    winter breaks up,
Love-buds put before you and within you
    whoever you are,
Buds to be unfolded on the old terms,
If you bring the warmth of the sun to
    them they will open and bring form,
    color, perfume, to you,
If you become the aliment and the wet
    they will become flowers, fruits, tall
    branches and trees.

1860

I SAW IN LOUISIANA A LIVE-OAK GROWING

I saw in Louisiana a live-oak growing,
All alone stood it and the moss hung
    down from the branches,
Without any companion it grew there
    uttering joyous leaves of dark green,
And its look, rude, unbending, lusty,
    made me think of myself,
But I wonder'd how it could utter joyous
    leaves standing alone there without its
    friend near, for I knew I could not,
And I broke off a twig with a certain
    number of leaves upon it, and twined
    around it a little moss,
And brought it away, and I have placed it
    in sight in my room,
It is not needed to remind me as of my
    own dear friends,
(For I believe lately I think of little else
    than of them,)
Yet it remains to me a curious token, it
    makes me think of manly love;
For all that, and though the live-oak
    glistens there in Louisiana solitary in
    a wide flat space,
Uttering joyous leaves all its life without a
    friend a lover near,
I know very well I could not.

1860

TO A STRANGER

Passing stranger! you do not know how
    longingly I look upon you,
You must be he I was seeking, or she I
    was seeking, (it comes to me as of a
    dream,)
I have somewhere surely lived a life of joy
    with you,
All is recall'd as we flit by each other,
    fluid, affectionate, chaste, matured,
You grew up with me, were a boy with
    me or a girl with me,
I ate with you and slept with you, your
    body has become not yours only nor
    left my body mine only,
You give me the pleasure of your eyes,
    face, flesh, as we pass, you take of my
    beard, breast, hands, in return,
I am not to speak to you, I am to think of
    you when I sit alone or wake at night
    alone,
I am to wait, I do not doubt I am to
    meet you again,
I am to see to it that I do not lose you.

1860

17

A GLIMPSE

A glimpse through an interstice caught,
Of a crowd of workmen and drivers in a
   bar-room around the stove late of a
   winter night, and I unremark'd seated
   in a corner,
Of a youth who loves me and whom I
   love, silently approaching and seating
   himself near, that he may hold me by
   the hand,
A long while amid the noises of coming
   and going, of drinking and oath and
   smutty jest,
There we two, content, happy in being
   together, speaking little, perhaps not
   a word.

1860

AMONG THE MULTITUDE

Among the men and women the
    multitude,
I perceive one picking me out by secret
    and divine signs,
Acknowledging none else, not parent,
    wife, husband, brother, child, any
    nearer than I am,
Some are baffled, but that one is not —
    that one knows me.

Ah lover and perfect equal,
I meant that you should discover me so
    by faint indirections,
And I when I meet you mean to discover
    you by the like in you.

1860

19

YOUTH, DAY, OLD AGE AND NIGHT

Youth, large, lusty, loving — youth full of
    grace, force, fascination,
Do you know that Old Age may come
    after you with equal grace, force,
    fascination?

Day full-blown and splendid — day of the
    immense sun, action, ambition,
    laughter,
The Night follows close with millions of
    suns, and sleep and restoring
    darkness.

1881

A NOISELESS PATIENT SPIDER

A noiseless patient spider,
I mark'd where on a little promontory it
    stood isolated,
Mark'd how to explore the vacant vast
    surrounding,
It launch'd forth filament, filament,
    filament, out of itself,
Ever unreeling them, ever tirelessly
    speeding them.

And you O my soul where you stand,
Surrounded, detached, in measureless
    oceans of space,
Ceaselessly musing, venturing, throwing,
    seeking the spheres to connect them,
Till the bridge you will need be form'd,
    till the ductile anchor hold,
Till the gossamer thread you fling catch
    somewhere, O my soul.

1868

ME IMPERTURBE

Me imperturbe, standing at ease in
  Nature,
Master of all or mistress of all, aplomb in
  the midst of irrational things,
Imbued as they, passive, receptive, silent
  as they,
Finding my occupation, poverty,
  notoriety, foibles, crimes, less
  important than I thought,
Me toward the Mexican sea, or in the
  Mannahatta or the Tennessee, or far
  north or inland,
A river man, or a man of the woods, or of
  any farm-life of these States or of the
  coast, or the lakes or Kanada,
Me wherever my life is lived, O to be self-
  balanced for contingencies,
To confront night, storms, hunger,
  ridicule, accidents, rebuffs, as the
  trees and animals do.

1860

MY PICTURE-GALLERY

In a little house keep I pictures
    suspended, it is not a fix'd house,
It is round, it is only a few inches from
    one side to the other;
Yet behold, it has room for all the shows
    of the world, all memories!
Here the tableaus of life, and here the
    groupings of death;
Here, do you know this? this is cicerone
    himself,
With finger rais'd he points to the prodigal
    pictures.

1880

A HAND-MIRROR

Hold it up sternly — see this it sends
    back, (who is it? is it you?)
Outside fair costume, within ashes and
    filth,
No more a flashing eye, no more a
    sonorous voice or springy step,
Now some slave's eye, voice, hands, step,
A drunkard's breath, unwholesome eater's
    face, venerealee's flesh,
Lungs rotting away piecemeal, stomach
    sour and cankerous,
Joints rheumatic, bowels clogged with
    abomination,
Blood circulating dark and poisonous
    streams,
Words babble, hearing and touch callous,
No brain, no heart left, no magnetism of
    sex;
Such from one look in this looking-glass
    ere you go hence,
Such a result so soon — and from such a
    beginning!

1860

HALCYON DAYS

Not from successful love alone,
Nor wealth, nor honor'd middle age, nor
    victories of politics or war;
But as life wanes, and all the turbulent
    passions calm,
As gorgeous, vapory, silent hues cover the
    evening sky,
As softness, fulness, rest, suffuse the
    frame, like fresher, balmier air,
As the days take on a mellower light, and
    the apple at last hangs really finish'd
    and indolent-ripe on the tree,
Then for the teeming quietest, happiest
    days of all!
The brooding and blissful halcyon days!

1888

THE DALLIANCE OF THE EAGLES

Skirting the river road, (my forenoon
    walk, my rest,)
Skyward in air a sudden muffled sound,
    the dalliance of the eagles,
The rushing amorous contact high in
    space together,
The clinching interlocking claws, a living,
    fierce, gyrating wheel,
Four beating wings, two beaks, a swirling
    mass tight grappling,
In tumbling turning clustering loops,
    straight downward falling,
Till o'er the river pois'd, the twain yet
    one, a moment's lull,
A motionless still balance in the air, then
    parting, talons loosing,
Upward again on slow-firm pinions
    slanting, their separate diverse flight,
She hers, he his, pursuing.

1880

OLD SALT KOSSABONE

Far back, related on my mother's
    side,
Old Salt Kossabone, I'll tell you how he
    died:
(Had been a sailor all his life — was
    nearly 90 — lived with his married
    grandchild, Jenny;
House on a hill, with view of bay at hand,
    and distant cape, and stretch to open
    sea;)
The last of afternoons, the evening
    hours, for many a year his regular
    custom,
In his great arm chair by the window
    seated,
(Sometimes, indeed, through half the
    day,)
Watching the coming, going of the
    vessels, he mutters to himself — And
    now the close of all:
One struggling outbound brig, one day,
    baffled for long — cross-tides and
    much wrong going,
At last at nightfall strikes the breeze
    aright, her whole luck veering,
And swiftly bending round the cape, the
    darkness proudly entering, cleaving,
    as he watches,

'She's free — she's on her destination' —
   these the last words — when Jenny
   came, he sat there dead,
Dutch Kossabone, Old Salt, related on
   my mother's side, far back.

                                    1888

A TWILIGHT SONG

As I sit in twilight late alone by the
    flickering oak flame,
Musing on long-pass'd war-scenes — of
    the countless buried unknown soldiers,
Of the vacant names, as unindented air's
    and sea's — the unreturn'd,
The brief truce after battle, with grim
    burial-squads, and the deep-fill'd
    trenches,
Of gather'd dead from all America,
    North, South, East, West, whence
    they came up,
From wooded Maine, New-England's
    farms, from fertile Pennsylvania,
    Illinois, Ohio,
From the measureless West, Virginia, the
    South, the Carolinas, Texas,
(Even here in my room-shadows and
    half-lights in the noiseless flickering
    flames,
Again I see the stalwart ranks on-filing,
    rising — I hear the rhythmic tramp
    of the armies;)
You million unwrit names all, all —
    you dark bequest from all the war,
A special verse for you — a flash of duty
    long neglected — your mystic roll
    strangely gather'd here,

Each name recall'd by me from out the
    darkness and death's ashes,
Henceforth to be, deep, deep within my
    heart recording, for many a future year,
Your mystic roll entire of unknown
    names, or North or South,
Embalm'd with love in this twilight song.

1890

THE RUNNER

On a flat road runs the well-train'd runner,
He is lean and sinewy with muscular legs,
He is thinly clothed, he leans forward as
    he runs,
With lightly closed fists and arms
    partially rais'd.

1867

PERFECTIONS

Only themselves understand themselves
    and the like of themselves,
As souls only understand souls.

1860

30

O TAN-FACED PRAIRIE-BOY

O tan-faced prairie-boy,
Before you came to camp came many a
     welcome gift,
Praises and presents came and nourishing
     food, till at last among the recruits,
You came, taciturn, with nothing to give
     — we but look'd on each other,
When lo! more than all the gifts of the
     world you gave me.

                                        1865

SOMETIMES WITH ONE I LOVE

Sometimes with one I love I fill myself
     with rage for fear I effuse unreturn'd
     love,
But now I think there is no unreturn'd
     love, the pay is certain one way or
     another,
(I loved a certain person ardently and my
     love was not return'd,
Yet out of that I have written these
     songs.)

                                        1860

WHOEVER YOU ARE HOLDING ME NOW IN HAND

Whoever you are holding me now in
     hand,
Without one thing all will be useless,
I give you fair warning before you
     attempt me further,
I am not what you supposed, but far
     different.

Who is he that would become my
     follower?
Who would sign himself a candidate for
     my affections?

The way is suspicious, the result
     uncertain, perhaps destructive,
You would have to give up all else, I
     alone would expect to be your sole
     and exclusive standard,
Your novitiate would even then be long
     and exhausting,
The whole past theory of your life and all
     conformity to the lives around you
     would have to be abandon'd,
Therefore release me now before
     troubling yourself any further, let go
     your hand from my shoulders,
Put me down and depart on your way.

Or else by stealth in some wood for
    trial,
Or back of a rock in the open air,
(For in any roof'd room of a house I
    emerge not, nor in company,
And in libraries I lie as one dumb, a
    gawk, or unborn, or dead,)
But just possibly with you on a high hill,
    first watching lest any person for
    miles around approach unawares,
Or possibly with you sailing at sea, or on
    the beach of the sea or some quiet
    island,
Here to put your lips upon mine I permit
    you,
With the comrade's long-dwelling kiss or
    the new husband's kiss,
For I am the new husband and I am the
    comrade.

Or if you will, thrusting me beneath your
    clothing,
Where I may feel the throbs of your heart
    or rest upon your hip,
Carry me when you go forth over land or
    sea;
For thus merely touching you is enough,
    is best,
And thus touching you would I silently
    sleep and be carried eternally.

But these leaves conning you con at peril,
For these leaves and me you will not
    understand,
They will elude you at first and still more
    afterward, I will certainly elude you,
Even while you should think you had
    unquestionably caught me, behold!
Already you see I have escaped from you.

For it is not for what I have put into it
    that I have written this book,
Nor is it by reading it you will acquire it,
Nor do those know me best who admire
    me and vauntingly praise me,
Nor will the candidates for my love
    (unless at most a very few) prove
    victorious,
Nor will my poems do good only, they
    will do just as much evil, perhaps
    more,
For all is useless without that which you
    may guess at many times and not hit,
    that which I hinted at;
Therefore release me and depart on your
    way.

1860

A SIGHT IN CAMP IN THE DAYBREAK GRAY AND DIM

A sight in camp in the daybreak gray and
dim,
As from my tent I emerge so early
sleepless,
As slow I walk in the cool fresh air the
path near by the hospital tent,
Three forms I see on stretchers lying,
brought out there untended lying,
Over each the blanket spread, ample
brownish woolen blanket,
Gray and heavy blanket, folding, covering
all.
Curious I halt and silent stand,
Then with light fingers I from the face of
the nearest the first just lift the
blanket;
Who are you elderly man so gaunt and
grim, with well-gray'd hair, and flesh
all sunken about the eyes?
Who are you my dear comrade?
Then to the second I step — and who are
you my child and darling?
Who are you sweet boy with cheeks yet
blooming?
Then to the third — a face nor child
nor old, very calm, as of beautiful
yellow-white ivory;

Young man I think I know you — I think
   this face is the face of the Christ
   himself,
Dead and divine and brother of all, and
   here again he lies.

1865

VIGIL STRANGE I KEPT ON THE FIELD ONE NIGHT

Vigil strange I kept on the field one
    night;
When you my son and my comrade dropt
    at my side that day,
One look I but gave which your dear eyes
    return'd with a look I shall never
    forget,
One touch of your hand to mine O boy,
    reach'd up as you lay on the ground,
Then onward I sped in the battle, the
    even-contested battle,
Till late in the night reliev'd to the place
    at last again I made my way,
Found you in death so cold dear
    comrade, found your body son of
    responding kisses, (never again on
    earth responding,)
Bared your face in the starlight, curious
    the scene, cool blew the moderate
    night-wind,
Long there and then in vigil I stood,
    dimly around me the battle-field
    spreading,
Vigil wondrous and vigil sweet there in
    the fragrant silent night,
But not a tear fell, not even a long-drawn
    sigh, long, long I gazed,

Then on the earth partially reclining sat
by your side leaning my chin in my
hands,
Passing sweet hours, immortal and mystic
hours with you dearest comrade —
not a tear, not a word,
Vigil of silence, love and death, vigil for
you my son and my soldier,
As onward silently stars aloft, eastward
new ones upward stole,
Vigil final for you brave boy, (I could not
save you, swift was your death,
I faithfully loved you and cared for you
living, I think we shall surely meet
again,)
Till at latest lingering of the
night, indeed just as the dawn
appear'd,
My comrade I wrapt in his blanket,
envelop'd well his form,
Folded the blanket well, tucking it
carefully over head and carefully
under feet,
And there and then and bathed by the
rising sun, my son in his grave, in his
rude-dug grave I deposited,
Ending my vigil strange with that, vigil of
night and battle-field dim,
Vigil for boy of responding kisses,
(never again on earth responding,)

Vigil for comrade swiftly slain, vigil I
    never forget, how as day brighten'd,
I rose from the chill ground and folded
    my soldier well in his blanket,
And buried him where he fell.

1865

AN ARMY CORPS ON THE MARCH

With its cloud of skirmishers in advance,
With now the sound of a single shot
    snapping like a whip, and now an
    irregular volley,
The swarming ranks press on and on,
    the dense brigades press on,
Glittering dimly, toiling under the sun —
    the dustcover'd men,
In columns rise and fall to the
    undulations of the ground,
With artillery interspers'd — the wheels
    rumble, the horses sweat,
As the army corps advances.

1865–6

CAVALRY CROSSING A FORD

A line in long array where they wind
    betwixt green islands,
They take a serpentine course, their arms
    flash in the sun — hark to the
    musical clank,
Behold the silvery river, in it the
    splashing horses loitering stop to
    drink,
Behold the brown-faced men, each group,
    each person a picture, the negligent
    rest on the saddles,
Some emerge on the opposite bank,
    others are just entering the ford —
    while,
Scarlet and blue and snowy white,
The guidon flags flutter gayly in the
    wind.

1865

THE WOUND-DRESSER

I

An old man bending I come among
    new faces,
Years looking backward resuming in
    answer to children,
Come tell us old man, as from young
    men and maidens that love me,
(Arous'd and angry, I'd thought to beat
    the alarum, and urge relentless war,
But soon my fingers fail'd me, my face
    droop'd and I resign'd myself,
To sit by the wounded and soothe them,
    or silently watch the dead;)
Years hence of these scenes, of these
    furious passions, these chances,
Of unsurpass'd heroes, (was one side so
    brave? the other was equally brave;)
Now be witness again, paint the mightiest
    armies of earth,
Of those armies so rapid so wondrous
    what saw you to tell us?
What stays with you latest and deepest?
    of curious panics,
Of hard-fought engagements or sieges
    tremendous what deepest remains?

II

O maidens and young men I love and
    that love me,
What you ask of my days those the
    strangest and sudden your talking
    recalls,
Soldiers alert I arrive after a long march
    cover'd with sweat and dust,
In the nick of time I come, plunge in the
    fight, loudly shout in the rush of
    successful charge,
Enter the captur'd works — yet lo, like a
    swift-running river they fade,
Pass and are gone they fade — I dwell
    not on soldiers' perils or soldiers'
    joys,
(Both I remember well — many the
    hardships, few the joys, yet I was
    content.)

But in silence, in dreams' projections,
While the world of gain and appearance
    and mirth goes on,
So soon what is over forgotten,
    and waves wash the imprints off
    the sand,
With hinged knees returning I enter the
    doors, (while for you up there,
Whoever you are, follow without noise
    and be of strong heart.)

Bearing the bandages, water and sponge,
Straight and swift to my wounded I go,
Where they lie on the ground after the
    battle brought in,
Where their priceless blood reddens the
    grass the ground,
Or to the rows of the hospital tent, or
    under the roof'd hospital,
To the long rows of cots up and down
    each side I return,
To each and all one after another I draw
    near, not one do I miss,
An attendant follows holding a tray, he
    carries a refuse pail,
Soon to be fill'd with clotted rags and
    blood, emptied, and fill'd again.

I onward go, I stop,
With hinged knees and steady hand to
    dress wounds,
I am firm with each, the pangs are sharp
    yet unavoidable,
One turns to me his appealing eyes —
    poor boy! I never knew you,
Yet I think I could not refuse this
    moment to die for you, if that would
    save you.

III

On, on I go, (open doors of time! open
    hospital doors!)
The crush'd head I dress, (poor crazed
    hand tear not the bandage away,)
The neck of the cavalry-man with the
    bullet through and through I
    examine,
Hard the breathing rattles, quite glazed
    already the eye, yet life struggles
    hard,
(Come sweet death! be persuaded O
    beautiful death!
In mercy come quickly.)

From the stump of the arm, the
    amputated hand,
I undo the clotted lint, remove the
    slough, wash off the matter and
    blood,
Back on his pillow the soldier bends with
    curv'd neck and side-falling head,
His eyes are closed, his face is pale, he
    dares not look on the bloody stump,
And has not yet look'd on it.

I dress a wound in the side, deep, deep,
But a day or two more, for see the frame
    all wasted and sinking,
And the yellow-blue countenance see.

44

I dress the perforated shoulder, the foot
with the bullet-wound,
Cleanse the one with a gnawing and
putrid gangrene, so sickening, so
offensive,
While the attendant stands behind aside
me holding the tray and pail.

I am faithful, I do not give out,
The fractur'd thigh, the knee, the wound
in the abdomen,
These and more I dress with impassive
hand, (yet deep in my breast a fire, a
burning flame.)

IV

Thus in silence in dreams' projections,
Returning, resuming, I thread my way
through the hospitals,
The hurt and wounded I pacify with
soothing hand,
I sit by the restless all the dark night,
some are so young,
Some suffer so much, I recall the
experience sweet and sad,
(Many a soldier's loving arms about this
neck have cross'd and rested,
Many a soldier's kiss dwells on these
bearded lips.)

1865

RECONCILIATION

Word over all, beautiful as the sky,
Beautiful that war and all its deeds of
    carnage must in time be utterly lost,
That the hands of the sisters Death and
    Night incessantly softly wash again,
    and ever again, this soil'd world;
For my enemy is dead, a man divine as
    myself is dead,
I look where he lies white-faced and still
    in the coffin — I draw near,
Bend down and touch lightly with my lips
    the white face in the coffin.

1865–6

AS I LAY WITH MY HEAD IN YOUR LAP CAMERADO

As I lay with my head in your lap
    camerado,
The confession I made I resume, what I
    said to you and the open air I resume,
I know I am restless and make others so,
I know my words are weapons full of
    danger, full of death,
For I confront peace, security and all the
    settled laws, to unsettle them,
I am more resolute because all have
    denied me than I could ever have
    been had all accepted me,
I heed not and have never heeded either
    experience, cautions, majorities, nor
    ridicule,
And the threat of what is call'd hell is
    little or nothing to me,
And the lure of what is call'd heaven is
    little or nothing to me;
Dear camerado! I confess I have urged
    you onward with me, and still urge
    you, without the least idea what is
    our destination,
Or whether we shall be victorious, or
    utterly quell'd and defeated.

1865–6

47

CROSSING BROOKLYN FERRY

I

Flood-tide below me! I see you face to
face!

Clouds of the west — sun there half an
hour high — I see you also face to
face.

Crowds of men and women attired in the
usual costumes, how curious you are
to me!

On the ferry-boats the hundreds and
hundreds that cross, returning home,
are more curious to me than you
suppose,

And you that shall cross from shore to
shore years hence are more to me,
and more in my meditations, than
you might suppose.

II

The impalpable sustenance of me from all
things at all hours of the day,

The simple, compact, well-join'd scheme,
myself disintegrated, every one
disintegrated yet part of the
scheme,

The similitudes of the past and those of
the future,

The glories strung like beads on my
    smallest sights and hearings, on the
    walk in the street and the passage
    over the river,
The current rushing so swiftly and
    swimming with me far away,
The others that are to follow me, the ties
    between me and them,
The certainty of others, the life, love,
    sight, hearing of others.

Others will enter the gates of the ferry
    and cross from shore to shore,
Others will watch the run of the flood-
    tide,
Others will see the shipping of Manhattan
    north and west, and the heights of
    Brooklyn to the south and east,
Others will see the islands large and
    small;
Fifty years hence, others will see them as
    they cross, the sun half an hour high,
A hundred years hence, or ever so many
    hundred years hence, others will see
    them,
Will enjoy the sunset, the pouring-in of
    the flood-tide, the falling-back to the
    sea of the ebb-tide.

It avails not, time nor place — distance
    avails not,
I am with you, you men and women of a
    generation, or ever so many
    generations hence,
Just as you feel when you look on the
    river and sky, so I felt,
Just as any of you is one of a living
    crowd, I was one of a crowd,
Just as you are refresh'd by the gladness
    of the river and the bright flow, I was
    refresh'd,
Just as you stand and lean on the rail, yet
    hurry with the swift current, I stood
    yet was hurried,
Just as you look on the numberless masts
    of ships and the thick-stemm'd pipes
    of steamboats, I look'd.
I too many and many a time cross'd the
    river of old,
Watched the Twelfth-month sea-gulls, saw
    them high in the air floating with
    motionless wings, oscillating their
    bodies,
Saw how the glistening yellow lit up parts
    of their bodies and left the rest in
    strong shadow,
Saw the slow-wheeling circles and the
    gradual edging towards the south,

Saw the reflection of the summer sky in
the water,
Had my eyes dazzled by the shimmering
track of beams,
Look'd at the fine centrifugal spokes of
light round the shape of my head in
the sunlit water,
Look'd on the haze on the hills
southward and south-westward,
Look'd on the vapor as it flew in fleeces
tinged with violet,
Look'd toward the lower bay to notice the
vessels arriving,
Saw their approach, saw aboard those
that were near me,
Saw the white sails of schooners and
sloops, saw the ships at anchor,
The sailors at work in the rigging or out
astride the spars,
The round masts, the swinging motion of
the hulls, the slender serpentine
pennants,
The large and small steamers in motion,
the pilots in their pilot-houses,
The white wake left by the passage, the
quick tremulous whirl of the
wheels,
The flags of all nations, the falling of
them at sunset,
The scallop-edged waves in the twilight,

the ladled cups, the frolicsome crests
and glistening,
The stretch afar growing dimmer and
dimmer, the gray walls of the granite
storehouses by the docks,
On the river the shadowy group, the big
steam-tug closely flank'd on each side
by the barges, the hay-boat, the
belated lighter,
On the neighboring shore the fires from
the foundry chimneys burning high
and glaringly into the night,
Casting their flicker of black contrasted
with wild red and yellow light over
the tops of houses, and down into the
clefts of streets.

IV

These and all else were to me the same
as they are to you,
I loved well those cities, loved well the
stately and rapid river,
The men and women I saw were all near
to me,
Others the same — others who look back
on me because I look'd forward to
them,
(The time will come, though I stop here
to-day and to-night.)

V

What is it then between us?
What is the count of the scores or
    hundreds of years between us?

Whatever it is, it avails not — distance
    avails not, and place avails not,
I too lived, Brooklyn of ample hills was
    mine,
I too walk'd the streets of Manhattan
    island, and bathed in the waters
    around it,
I too felt the curious abrupt questionings
    stir within me,
In the day among crowds of people
    sometimes they came upon me,
In my walks home late at night or as I lay
    in my bed they came upon me,
I too had been struck from the float
    forever held in solution,
I too had receiv'd identity by my body,
That I was I knew was of my body, and
    what I should be I knew I should be
    of my body.

VI

It is not upon you alone the dark patches
    fall,
The dark threw its patches down upon
    me also,

The best I had done seem'd to me blank
 and suspicious,
My great thoughts as I supposed them,
 were they not in reality meagre?
Nor is it you alone who know what it is
 to be evil,
I am he who knew what it was to be evil,
I too knitted the old knot of contrariety,
Blabb'd, blush'd, resented, lied, stole,
 grudg'd,
Had guile, anger, lust, hot wishes I dared
 not speak,
Was wayward, vain, greedy, shallow, sly,
 cowardly, malignant,
The wolf, the snake, the hog, not wanting
 in me,
The cheating look, the frivolous word, the
 adulterous wish, not wanting,
Refusals, hates, postponements, meanness,
 laziness, none of these wanting,
Was one with the rest, the days and haps
 of the rest,
Was call'd by my nighest name by clear
 loud voices of young men as they saw
 me approaching or passing,
Felt their arms on my neck as I stood, or
 the negligent leaning of their flesh
 against me as I sat,
Saw many I loved in the street or
 ferry-boat or public assembly, yet

never told them a word,
Lived the same life with the rest,
    the same old laughing, gnawing,
    sleeping,
Play'd the part that still looks back on the
    actor or actress,
The same old role, the role that is what
    we make it, as great as we like,
Or as small as we like, or both great and
    small.

VII

Closer yet I approach you,
What thought you have of me now, I had
    as much of you — I laid in my stores
    in advance,
I consider'd long and seriously of you
    before you were born.

Who was to know what should come
    home to me?
Who knows but I am enjoying this?
Who knows, for all the distance, but I am
    as good as looking at you now, for all
    you cannot see me?

VIII

Ah, what can ever be more stately and
    admirable to me than mast-hemm'd
    Manhattan?

River and sunset and scallop-edg'd waves
of flood-tide?
The sea-gulls oscillating their bodies, the
hay-boat in the twilight, and the
belated lighter?
What gods can exceed these that clasp me
by the hand, and with voices I love
call me promptly and loudly by my
nighest name as I approach?
What is more subtle than this which ties
me to the woman or man that looks
in my face?
Which fuses me into you now, and pours
my meaning into you?

We understand then do we not?
What I promis'd without mentioning it,
have you not accepted?
What the study could not teach — what
the preaching could not accomplish is
accomplish'd, is it not?

IX
Flow on, river! flow with the flood-tide,
and ebb with the ebb-tide!
Frolic on, crested and scallop-edg'd
waves!
Gorgeous clouds of the sunset! drench
with your splendor me, or the men
and women generations after me!

Cross from shore to shore, countless
   crowds of passengers!
Stand up, tall masts of Mannahatta! stand
   up, beautiful hills of Brooklyn!
Throb, baffled and curious brain! throw
   out questions and answers!
Suspend here and everywhere, eternal
   float of solution!
Gaze, loving and thirsting eyes, in the
   house or street or public assembly!
Sound out, voices of young men! loudly
   and musically call me by my nighest
   name!
Live, old life! play the part that looks
   back on the actor or actress!
Play the old role, the role that is great or
   small according as one makes it!
Consider, you who peruse me, whether I
   may not in unknown ways be looking
   upon you;
Be firm, rail over the river, to support
   those who lean idly, yet haste with
   the hasting current;
Fly on, sea-birds! fly sideways, or wheel
   in large circles high in the air;
Receive the summer sky, you water, and
   faithfully hold it till all downcast eyes
   have time to take it from you!
Diverge, fine spokes of light, from the
   shape of my head, or any one's

head, in the sunlit water!
Come on, ships from the lower bay! pass
    up or down, white-sail'd schooners,
    sloops, lighters!
Flaunt away, flags of all nations! be duly
    lower'd at sunset!
Burn high your fires, foundry chimneys!
    cast black shadows at nightfall! cast
    red and yellow light over the tops of
    the houses!
Appearances, now or henceforth, indicate
    what you are,
You necessary film, continue to envelop
    the soul,
About my body for me, and your body
    for you, be hung our divinest aromas,
Thrive, cities — bring your freight, bring
    your shows, ample and sufficient
    rivers,
Expand, being than which none else is
    perhaps more spiritual,
Keep your places, objects than which
    none else is more lasting.

You have waited, you always wait, you
    dumb, beautiful ministers
We receive you with free sense at last,
    and are insatiate henceforward,
Not you any more shall be able to foil us,
    or withhold yourselves from us,

We use you, and do not cast you aside —
    we plant you permanently within us,

We fathom you not — we love you —
    there is perfection in you also,
You furnish your parts toward eternity,
Great or small, you furnish your parts
    toward the soul.

1856

THERE WAS A CHILD WENT FORTH

There was a child went forth every day,
And the first object he look'd upon, that
    object he became,
And that object became part of him for
    the day or a certain part of the day,
Or for many years or stretching cycles of
    years.

The early lilacs became part of this
    child,
And grass and white and red
    morning-glories, and white and
    red clover, and the song of the
    phœbe-bird,
And the Third-month lambs and the
    sow's pink-faint litter, and the mare's
    foal and the cow's calf,
And the noisy brood of the barnyard or
    by the mire of the pondside,
And the fish suspending themselves so
    curiously below there, and the
    beautiful curious liquid,
And the water-plants with their graceful
    flat heads, all became part of him.

The field-sprouts of Fourth-month and
    Fifth-month became part of him,

Winter-grain sprouts and those of the
     light-yellow corn, and the esculent
     roots of the garden,
And the apple-trees cover'd with
     blossoms and the fruit afterward, and
     wood-berries, and the commonest
     weeds by the road,
And the old drunkard staggering home
     from the outhouse of the tavern
     whence he had lately risen,
And the schoolmistress that pass'd on her
     way to the school,
And the friendly boys that pass'd, and the
     quarrelsome boys,
And the tidy and fresh-cheek'd girls, and
     the barefoot negro boy and girl,
And all the changes of city and country
     wherever he went.

His own parents, he that had father'd
     him and she that had conceiv'd him
     in her womb and birth'd him,
They gave this child more of themselves
     than that,
They gave him afterward every day, they
     became part of him.
The mother at home quietly placing the
     dishes on the supper-table,
The mother with mild words, clean her
     cap and gown, a wholesome odor

falling off her person and clothes as
she walks by,
The father, strong, self-sufficient, manly,
mean, anger'd, unjust,
The blow, the quick loud word, the tight
bargain, the crafty lure,
The family usages, the language, the
company, the furniture, the yearning
and swelling heart,
Affection that will not be gainsay'd, the
sense of what is real, the thought if
after all it should prove unreal,
The doubts of day-time and the doubts of
night-time, the curious whether and
how,
Whether that which appears so is so, or is
it all flashes and specks?
Men and women crowding fast in the
streets, if they are not flashes and
specks what are they?
The streets themselves and the façades of
houses, and goods in the windows,
Vehicles, teams, the heavy-plank'd
wharves, the huge crossing at the
ferries,
The village on the highland seen from
afar at sunset, the river between,

Shadows, aureola and mist, the light
falling on roofs and gables of white or

brown two miles off,

The schooner near by sleepily dropping
down the tide, the little boat
slack-tow'd astern,

The hurrying tumbling waves,
quick-broken crests, slapping,

The strata of color'd clouds, the long bar
of maroon-tint away solitary by itself,
the spread of purity it lies motionless
in,

The horizon's edge, the flying sea-crow,
the fragrance of salt marsh and shore
mud,

These became part of that child who
went forth every day, and who now
goes, and will always go forth every
day.

1855

STARTING FROM PAUMANOK

I

Starting from fish-shape Paumanok where
    I was born,
Well-begotten, and rais'd by a perfect
    mother,
After roaming many lands, lover of
    populous pavements,
Dweller in Mannahatta my city, or on
    southern savannas,
Or a soldier camp'd or carrying my
    knapsack and gun, or a miner in
    California,
Or rude in my home in Dakota's woods,
    my diet meat, my drink from the spring,
Or withdrawn to muse and meditate in
    some deep recess,
Far from the clank of crowds intervals
    passing rapt and happy,
Aware of the fresh free giver the flowing
    Missouri, aware of mighty Niagara,
Aware of the buffalo herds grazing
    the plains, the hirsute and
    strong-breasted bull,
Of earth, rocks, Fifth-month flowers
    experienced, stars, rain, snow, my
    amaze,
Having studied the mocking-bird's tones
    and the flight of the mountain-hawk,

64

And heard at dawn the unrivall'd one,
    the hermit thrush from the
    swamp-cedars,
Solitary, singing in the West, I strike up
    for a New World.

II
Victory, union, faith, identity, time,
The indissoluble compacts, riches,
    mystery,
Eternal progress, the kosmos, and the
    modern reports.

This then is life,
Here is what has come to the surface
    after so many throes and convulsions.

How curious! how real!
Underfoot the divine soil, overhead the
    sun.

See revolving the globe,
The ancestor-continents away group'd
    together,
The present and future continents north
    and south, with the isthmus between.

See, vast trackless spaces,
As in a dream they change, they swiftly
    fill,

Countless masses debouch upon them,
They are now cover'd with the foremost
    people, arts, institutions, known.

See, projected through time,
For me an audience interminable.
With firm and regular step they wend,
    they never stop,
Successions of men, Americanos, a
    hundred millions,
One generation playing its part and
    passing on,
Another generation playing its part and
    passing on in its turn,
With faces turn'd sideways or backward
    towards me to listen,
With eyes retrospective towards me.

III

Americanos! conquerors! marches
    humanitarian!
Foremost! century marches! Libertad!
    masses!
For you a programme of chants.

Chants of the prairies,
Chants of the long-running Mississippi,
    and down to the Mexican sea,
Chants of Ohio, Indiana, Illinois, Iowa,
    Wisconsin and Minnesota,

Chants going forth from the centre from
     Kansas, and thence equidistant,
Shooting in pulses of fire ceaseless to
     vivify all.

IV

Take my leaves America, take them South
     and take them North,
Make welcome for them everywhere, for
     they are your own offspring,
Surround them East and West, for they
     would surround you,
And you precedents, connect lovingly
     with them, for they connect lovingly
     with you.

I conn'd old times,
I sat studying at the feet of the great
     masters,
Now if eligible O that the great masters
     might return and study me.

In the name of these States shall I scorn
     the antique?
Why these are the children of the antique
     to justify it.

V

Dead poets, philosophs, priests,
Martyrs, artists, inventors, governments
     long since,

Language-shapers on other shores,
Nations once powerful, now reduced,
    withdrawn, or desolate,
I dare not proceed till I respectfully credit
    what you have left wafted hither,
I have perused it, own it is admirable,
    (moving awhile among it,)
Think nothing can ever be greater,
    nothing can ever deserve more than it
    deserves,
Regarding it all intently a long while,
    then dismissing it,
I stand in my place with my own day here.

Here lands female and male,
Here the heir-ship and heiress-ship of the
    world, here the flame of materials,
Here spirituality the translatress, the
    openly-avow'd,
The ever-tending, the finalè of visible
    forms,
The satisfier, after due long-waiting now
    advancing,
Yes here comes my mistress the soul.

VI

The soul,
Forever and forever — longer than soil is
    brown and solid — longer than water
    ebbs and flows.

I will make the poems of materials, for I
     think they are to be the most spiritual
     poems,
And I will make the poems of my body
     and of mortality,
For I think I shall then supply myself
     with the poems of my soul and of
     immortality.
I will make a song for these States that no
     one State may under any circumstances
     be subjected to another State,
And I will make a song that there shall be
     comity by day and by night between
     all the States, and between any two of
     them,
And I will make a song for the ears of the
     President, full of weapons with
     menacing points,
And behind the weapons countless
     dissatisfied faces;
And a song make I of the One form'd out
     of all,
The fang'd and glittering One whose head
     is over all,
Resolute warlike One including and over
     all,
(However high the head of any else that
     head is over all.)

I will acknowledge contemporary lands,

I will trail the whole geography of the
   globe and salute courteously every
   city large and small,
And employments! I will put in my
   poems that with you is heroism upon
   land and sea,
And I will report all heroism from an
   American point of view.

I will sing the song of companionship,
I will show what alone must finally
   compact these,
I believe these are to found their own ideal
   of manly love, indicating it in me,
I will therefore let flame from me the
   burning fires that were threatening to
   consume me,
I will lift what has too long kept down
   those smouldering fires,
I will give them complete abandonment,
I will write the evangel-poem of comrades
   and of love,
For who but I should understand love
   with all its sorrow and joy?
And who but I should be the poet of
   comrades?

VII
I am the credulous man of qualities, ages,
   races,

I advance from the people in their own
    spirit,
Here is what sings unrestricted faith.

Omnes! omnes! let others ignore what
    they may,
I make the poem of evil also, I
    commemorate that part also,
I am myself just as much evil as good,
    and my nation is — and I say there is
    in fact no evil,
(Or if there is I say it is just as important
    to you, to the land or to me, as
    anything else.)

I too, following many and follow'd by
    many, inaugurate a religion, I descend
    into the arena,
(It may be I am destin'd to utter the
    loudest cries there, the winner's
    pealing shouts,
Who knows? they may rise from me yet,
    and soar above every thing.)

Each is not for its own sake,
I say the whole earth and all the stars in
    the sky are for religion's sake.

I say no man has ever yet been half
    devout enough,

None has ever yet adored or worship'd
      half enough,
None has begun to think how divine he
      himself is, and how certain the future
      is.

I say that the real and permanent
      grandeur of these States must be
      their religion,
Otherwise there is no real and permanent
      grandeur;
(Nor character nor life worthy the name
      without religion,
Nor land nor man or woman without
      religion.)

VIII

What are you doing young man?
Are you so earnest, so given up to
      literature, science, art, amours?
These ostensible realities, politics,
      points?
Your ambition or business whatever it
      may be?

It is well — against such I say not a
      word, I am their poet also,
But behold! such swiftly subside, burnt
      up for religion's sake,
For not all matter is fuel to heat,

impalpable flame, the essential life of
the earth,
Any more than such are to religion.

IX

What do you seek so pensive and silent?
What do you need camerado?
Dear son do you think it is love?
Listen dear son — listen America,
daughter or son,
It is a painful thing to love a man or
woman to excess, and yet it satisfies,
it is great,
But there is something else very great, it
makes the whole coincide,
It, magnificent, beyond materials, with
continuous hands sweeps and
provides for all.

X

Know you, solely to drop in the earth the
germs of a greater religion,
The following chants each for its kind I
sing.
My comrade!
For you to share with me two greatnesses,
and a third one rising inclusive and
more resplendent,
The greatness of Love and Democracy,
and the greatness of Religion.

73

Melange mine own, the unseen and the
    seen,
Mysterious ocean where the streams
    empty,
Prophetic spirit of materials shifting and
    flickering around me,
Living beings, identities now doubtless
    near us in the air that we know not
    of,
Contact daily and hourly that will not
    release me,
These selecting, these in hints demanded
    of me.

Not he with a daily kiss onward from
    childhood kissing me,
Has winded and twisted around me that
    which holds me to him,
Any more than I am held to the heavens
    and all the spiritual world,
After what they have done to me,
    suggesting themes.

O such themes — equalities! O divine
    average!
Warblings under the sun, usher'd as now,
    or at noon, or setting,
Strains musical flowing through ages, now
    reaching hither,
I take to your reckless and composite

chords, add to them, and cheerfully
pass them forward.

XI

As I have walk'd in Alabama my morning
walk,
I have seen where the she-bird the
mocking-bird sat on her nest in the
briers hatching her brood.

I have seen the he-bird also,
I have paus'd to hear him near at hand
inflating his throat and joyfully singing.

And while I paus'd it came to me that
what he really sang for was not there
only,
Nor for his mate nor himself only, nor all
sent back by the echoes,
But subtle, clandestine, away beyond,
A charge transmitted and gift occult for
those being born.

XII

Democracy! near at hand to you a throat
is now inflating itself and joyfully
singing.

Ma femme! for the brood beyond us and
of us,

For those who belong here and those to
    come,
I exultant to be ready for them will now
    shake out carols stronger and
    haughtier than have ever yet been
    heard upon earth.

I will make the songs of passions to give
    them their way,
And your songs outlaw'd offenders, for I
    scan you with kindred eyes, and carry
    you with me the same as any.

I will make the true poem of riches,
To earn for the body and the mind
    whatever adheres and goes forward
    and is not dropt by death;
I will effuse egotism and show it
    underlying all, and I will be the bard
    of personality,
And I will show of male and female that
    either is but the equal of the other,
And sexual organs and acts! do you
    concentrate in me, for I am
    determin'd to tell you with
    courageous clear voice to prove you
    illustrious,
And I will show that there is no
    imperfection in the present, and can
    be none in the future,

And I will show that whatever happens to
     anybody it may be turn'd to beautiful
     results,
And I will show that nothing can happen
     more beautiful than death,
And I will thread a thread through my
     poems that time and events are
     compact,
And that all the things of the universe are
     perfect miracles, each as profound as
     any.

I will not make poems with reference to
     parts,
But I will make poems, songs, thoughts,
     with reference to ensemble,
And I will not sing with reference to a
     day, but with reference to all days,
And I will not make a poem nor the least
     part of a poem but has reference to
     the soul,
Because having look'd at the objects of
     the universe, I find there is no one
     nor any particle of one but has
     reference to the soul.

XIII

Was somebody asking to see the soul?
See, your own shape and countenance,
     persons, substances, beasts, the trees,

the running rivers, the rocks and
    sands.

All hold spiritual joys and afterwards
    loosen them;
How can the real body ever die and be
    buried?

Of your real body and any man's or
    woman's real body,
Item for item it will elude the hands of
    the corpse-cleaners and pass to fitting
    spheres,
Carrying what has accrued to it from the
    moment of birth to the moment of
    death.

Not the types set up by the printer return
    their impression, the meaning, the
    main concern,
Any more than a man's substance and life
    or a woman's substance and life
    return in the body and the soul,
Indifferently before death and after death.

Behold, the body includes and is the
    meaning, the main concern, and
    includes and is the soul;
Whoever you are, how superb and how
    divine is your body, or any part of it!

XIV

Whoever you are, to you endless
    announcements!

Daughter of the lands did you wait for
    your poet?
Did you wait for one with a flowing
    mouth and indicative hand?
Toward the male of the States, and
    toward the female of the States,
Exulting words, words to Democracy's
    lands.
Interlinked, food-yielding lands!
Land of coal and iron! land of gold! land
    of cotton, sugar, rice!
Land of wheat, beef, pork! land of wool
    and hemp! land of the apple and the
    grape!
Land of the pastoral plains, the
    grass-fields of the world! land of
    those sweet-air'd interminable
    plateaus!
Land of the herd, the garden, the healthy
    house of adobie!
Lands where the north-west Columbia
    winds, and where the south-west
    Colorado winds!
Land of the eastern Chesapeake! land of
    the Delaware!
Land of Ontario, Erie, Huron, Michigan!

Land of the Old Thirteen! Massachusetts
    land! land of Vermont and
    Connecticut!
Land of the ocean shores! land of sierras
    and peaks!
Land of boatmen and sailors! fishermen's
    land!
Inextricable lands! the clutch'd together!
    the passionate ones!
The side by side! the elder and younger
    brothers! the bony-limb'd!
The great women's land! the feminine!
    the experienced sisters and the
    inexperienced sisters!
Far breath'd land! Arctic braced! Mexican
    breez'd! the diverse! the compact!
The Pennsylvanian! the Virginian! the
    double-Carolinian!
O all and each well-loved by me! my
    intrepid nations! O I at any rate
    include you all with perfect love!
I cannot be discharged from you! not
    from one any sooner than another!
O death! O for all that, I am yet of you
    unseen this hour with irrepressible
    love,
Walking New England, a friend, a
    traveler,
Splashing my bare feet in the edge of the
    summer ripples on Paumanok's sands,

Crossing the prairies, dwelling again in
   Chicago, dwelling in every town,
Observing shows, births, improvements,
   structures, arts,
Listening to orators and oratresses in
   public halls,
Of and through the States as during life,
   each man and woman my neighbor,
The Louisianian, the Georgian, as near to
   me, and I as near to him and her,
The Mississippian and Arkansian yet with
   me, and I yet with any of them,
Yet upon the plains west of the spinal
   river, yet in my house of adobie,
Yet returning eastward, yet in the Seaside
   State or in Maryland,
Yet Kanadian cheerily braving the winter,
   the snow and ice welcome to me,
Yet a true son either of Maine or of the
   Granite State, or the Narragansett
   Bay State, or the Empire State,
Yet sailing to other shores to annex the
   same, yet welcoming every new
   brother,
Hereby applying these leaves to the new
   ones from the hour they unite with
   the old ones,
Coming among the new ones myself to be
   their companion and equal, coming
   personally to you now,

Enjoining you to acts, characters,
    spectacles, with me.

XV

With me with firm holding, yet haste,
    haste on.

For your life adhere to me,
(I may have to be persuaded many times
    before I consent to give myself really
    to you, but what of that?
Must not Nature be persuaded many times?)

No dainty dolce affettuoso I,
Bearded, sun-burnt, gray-neck'd,
    forbidding, I have arrived,

To be wrestled with as I pass for the solid
    prizes of the universe,
For such I afford whoever can persevere
    to win them.

XVI

On my way a moment I pause,
Here for you! and here for America!
Still the present I raise aloft, still the
    future of the States I harbinge and
    glad and sublime,
And for the past I pronounce what the air
    holds of the red aborigines.

The red aborigines,
Leaving natural breaths, sounds of rain
 and winds, calls as of birds and
 animals in the woods, syllabled to us
 for names,
Okonee, Koosa, Ottawa, Monongahela,
 Sauk, Natchez, Chattahoochee,
 Kaqueta, Oronoco,
Wabash, Miami, Saginaw, Chippewa,
 Oshkosh, Walla-Walla,
Leaving such to the States they melt, they
 depart, charging the water and the
 land with names.

XVII

Expanding and swift, henceforth,
Elements, breeds, adjustments, turbulent,
 quick and audacious

A world primal again, vistas of glory
 incessant and branching,
A new race dominating previous ones and
 grander far, with new contests,
New politics, new literatures and
 religions, new inventions and arts.

These, my voice announcing — I will
 sleep no more but arise,
You oceans that have been calm within
 me! how I feel you, fathomless,

stirring, preparing unprecedented
waves and storms.

XVIII

See, steamers steaming through my
poems,
See, in my poem immigrants continually
coming and landing,
See, in arriere, the wigwam, the trail, the
hunter's hut, the flat-boat, the
maize-leaf, the claim, the rude fence,
and the backwoods village,
See, on the one side the Western Sea and
on the other the Eastern Sea, how
they advance and retreat upon my
poems as upon their own shores,
See, pastures and forests in my poems —
see, animals wild and tame — see,
beyond the Kaw, countless herds of
buffalo feeding on short curly grass,
See, in my poems, cities, solid, vast,
inland, with paved streets, with iron
and stone edifices, ceaseless vehicles,
and commerce,
See, the many-cylinder'd steam printing-
press — see, the electric telegraph
stretching across the continent,
See, through Atlantica's depths pulses
American Europe reaching, pulses of
Europe duly return'd,

See, the strong and quick locomotive
    as it departs, panting, blowing the
    steam-whistle,
See, ploughmen ploughing farms — see,
    miners digging mines — see, the
    numberless factories,
See, mechanics busy at their benches with
    tools — see from among them superior
    judges, philosophs, Presidents,
    emerge, drest in working dresses,
See, lounging through the shops and
    fields of the States, me well-belov'd,
    close-held by day and night,
Hear the loud echoes of my songs there
    — read the hints come at last.

XIX

O camerado close! O you and me at last,
    and us two only.
O a word to clear one's path ahead
    endlessly!
O something ecstatic and
    undemonstrable! O music wild!
O now I triumph — and you shall also;
O hand in hand — O wholesome pleasure
    — O one more desirer and lover!
O to haste firm holding — to haste, haste
    on with me.

1856

SONG OF MYSELF

I

I celebrate myself, and sing myself,
And what I assume you shall assume,
For every atom belonging to me as good
    belongs to you.

I loafe and invite my soul,
I lean and loafe at my ease observing a
    spear of summer grass.
My tongue, every atom of my blood,
    form'd from this soil, this air,
Born here of parents born here from
    parents the same, and their parents
    the same,
I, now thirty-seven years old in perfect
    health begin,
Hoping to cease not till death.

Creeds and schools in abeyance,
Retiring back a while sufficed at what
    they are, but never forgotten,
I harbor for good or bad, I permit to
    speak at every hazard,
Nature without check with original energy.

II

Houses and rooms are full of perfumes, the
    shelves are crowded with perfumes,

I breathe the fragrance myself and know
it and like it,
The distillation would intoxicate me also,
but I shall not let it.

The atmosphere is not a perfume, it has
no taste of the distillation, it is
odorless,
It is for my mouth forever, I am in love
with it,
I will go to the bank by the wood and
become undisguised and naked,
I am mad for it to be in contact with me.
The smoke of my own breath,
Echoes, ripples, buzz'd whispers,
love-root, silk-thread, crotch and vine,
My respiration and inspiration, the
beating of my heart, the passing of
blood and air through my lungs,
The sniff of green leaves and dry leaves,
and of the shore and dark-color'd
sea-rocks, and of hay in the barn,
The sound of the belch'd words of my
voice loos'd to the eddies of the wind,
A few light kisses, a few embraces, a
reaching around of arms,
The play of shine and shade on the trees
as the supple boughs wag,
The delight alone or in the rush of the
streets, or along the fields and hill-sides,

The feeling of health, the full-noon trill,
the song of me rising from bed and
meeting the sun.

Have you reckon'd a thousand acres
much? have you reckon'd the earth
much?
Have you practis'd so long to learn to
read?
Have you felt so proud to get at the
meaning of poems?

Stop this day and night with me and you
shall possess the origin of all poems,
You shall possess the good of the earth
and sun, (there are millions of suns
left,)
You shall no longer take things at second
or third hand, nor look through the
eyes of the dead, nor feed on the
spectres in books,
You shall not look through my eyes
either, nor take things from me,
You shall listen to all sides and filter them
from your self.

III
I have heard what the talkers were
talking, the talk of the beginning and
the end,

But I do not talk of the beginning or the
     end.

There was never any more inception than
     there is now,
Nor any more youth or age than there is
     now,
And will never be any more perfection
     than there is now,
Nor any more heaven or hell than there is
     now.

Urge and urge and urge,
Always the procreant urge of the world.

Out of the dimness opposite equals
     advance, always substance and
     increase, always sex,
Always a knit of identity, always
     distinction, always a breed of life.

To elaborate is no avail, learn'd and
     unlearn'd feel that it is so.

Sure as the most certain sure, plumb in
     the uprights, well entretied, braced in
     the beams,
Stout as a horse, affectionate, haughty,
     electrical,
I and this mystery here we stand.

Clear and sweet is my soul, and clear and sweet is all that is not my soul.

Lack one lacks both, and the unseen is proved by the seen,
Till that becomes unseen and receives proof in its turn.

Showing the best and dividing it from the worst age vexes age,
Knowing the perfect fitness and equanimity of things, while they discuss I am silent, and go bathe and admire myself.

Welcome is every organ and attribute of me, and of any man hearty and clean,
Not an inch nor a particle of an inch is vile, and none shall be less familiar than the rest.

I am satisfied — I see, dance, laugh, sing;
As the hugging and loving bed-fellow sleeps at my side through the night, and withdraws at the peep of the day with stealthy tread,
Leaving me baskets cover'd with white towels swelling the house with their plenty,

Shall I postpone my acceptation and
    realization and scream at my eyes,
That they turn from gazing after and
    down the road,
And forthwith cipher and show me to a
    cent,
Exactly the value of one and exactly the
    value of two, and which is ahead?

IV

Trippers and askers surround me,
People I meet, the effect upon me of my
    early life or the ward and city I live
    in, or the nation,
The latest dates, discoveries, inventions,
    societies, authors old and new,
My dinner, dress, associates, looks,
    compliments, dues,
The real or fancied indifference of some
    man or woman I love,
The sickness of one of my folks or of
    myself, or ill-doing or loss or lack of
    money, or depressions or
    exaltations,
Battles, the horrors of fratricidal war, the
    fever of doubtful news, the fitful
    events:
These come to me days and nights and
    go from me again,
But they are not the Me myself.

Apart from the pulling and hauling stands
    what I am,
Stands amused, complacent,
    compassionating, idle, unitary,
Looks down, is erect, or bends an arm on
    an impalpable certain rest,
Looking with side-curved head curious
    what will come next,
Both in and out of the game and
    watching and wondering at it.

Backward I see in my own days where I
    sweated through fog with linguists
    and contenders,
I have no mockings or arguments, I
    witness and wait.

V

I believe in you my soul, the other I am
    must not abase itself to you,
And you must not be abased to the other.
Loafe with me on the grass, loose the
    stop from your throat,
Not words, not music or rhyme I want, not
    custom or lecture, not even the best,
Only the lull I like, the hum of your
    valvèd voice.

I mind how once we lay such a
    transparent summer morning,

How you settled your head athwart my
  hips and gently turn'd over upon me,
And parted the shirt from my
  bosom-bone, and plunged your
  tongue to my bare-stript heart,
And reach'd till you felt my beard, and
  reach'd till you held my feet.
Swiftly arose and spread around me the
  peace and knowledge that pass all the
  argument of the earth,
And I know that the hand of God is the
  promise of my own,
And I know that the spirit of God is the
  brother of my own,
And that all the men ever born are also
  my brothers, and the women my
  sisters and lovers,

And that a kelson of the creation is love,
And limitless are leaves stiff or drooping
  in the fields,
And brown ants in the little wells beneath
  them,
And mossy scabs of the worm fence,
  heap'd stones, elder, mullein and
  poke-weed.

VI

A child said *What is the grass?* fetching
  it to me with full hands;

How could I answer the child? I do not
    know what it is any more than he.

I guess it must be the flag of my
    disposition, out of hopeful green stuff
    woven.

Or I guess it is the handkerchief of the
    Lord,
A scented gift and remembrancer
    designedly dropt,
Bearing the owner's name someway in the
    corners, that we may see and remark,
    and say *Whose?*

Or I guess the grass is itself a child, the
    produced babe of the vegetation.

Or I guess it is a uniform hieroglyphic,
And it means, Sprouting alike in broad
    zones and narrow zones,
Growing among black folks as among
    white,
Kanuck, Tuckahoe, Congressman, Cuff, I
    give them the same, I receive them
    the same.

And now it seems to me the beautiful
    uncut hair of graves.

Tenderly will I use you curling grass,
It may be you transpire from the breasts
of young men,
It may be if I had known them I would
have loved them,
It may be you are from old people, or
from offspring taken soon out of their
mothers' laps,
And here you are the mothers' laps.

This grass is very dark to be from the
white heads of old mothers,
Darker than the colorless beards of old
men,
Dark to come from under the faint red
roofs of mouths.

O I perceive after all so many uttering
tongues,
And I perceive they do not come from
the roofs of mouths for nothing.

I wish I could translate the hints about
the dead young men and women,
And the hints about old men and
mothers, and the offspring taken soon
out of their laps.

What do you think has become of the
young and old men?

And what do you think has become of the
women and children?

They are alive and well somewhere,
The smallest sprout shows there is really
no death,
And if ever there was it led forward life,
and does not wait at the end to arrest
it,
And ceas'd the moment life appear'd.

All goes onward and outward, nothing
collapses,
And to die is different from what any one
supposed, and luckier.

VII

Has any one supposed it lucky to be
born?
I hasten to inform him or her it is just as
lucky to die, and I know it.

I pass death with the dying and birth
with the newwash'd babe, and am
not contain'd between my hat and
boots,
And peruse manifold objects, no two alike
and every one good,
The earth good and the stars good, and
their adjuncts all good.

I am not an earth nor an adjunct of an
    earth,
I am the mate and companion of people,
    all just as immortal and fathomless as
    myself,
(They do not know how immortal, but I
    know.)

Every kind for itself and its own, for me
    mine male and female,
For me those that have been boys and
    that love women,
For me the man that is proud and feels
    how it stings to be slighted,
For me the sweet-heart and the old maid,
    for me mothers and the mothers of
    mothers,
For me lips that have smiled, eyes that
    have shed tears,
For me children and the begetters of
    children.

Undrape! you are not guilty to me, nor
    stale nor discarded,
I see through the broadcloth and gingham
    whether or no,
And am around, tenacious, acquisitive,
    tireless, and cannot be shaken away.

VIII

The little one sleeps in its cradle,
I lift the gauze and look a long time, and
    silently brush away flies with my
    hand.

The youngster and the red-faced girl turn
    aside up the busy hill,
I peeringly view them from the top.

The suicide sprawls on the bloody floor
    of the bedroom,
I witness the corpse with its dabbled
    hair, I note where the pistol has
    fallen.

The blab of the pave, tires of carts, sluff
    of boot-soles, talk of the
    promenaders,
The heavy omnibus, the driver with his
    interrogating thumb, the clank of the
    shod horses on the granite floor,
The snow-sleighs, clinking, shouted jokes,
    pelts of snow-balls,
The hurrahs for popular favorites, the
    fury of rous'd mobs,
The flap of the curtain'd litter, a sick man
    inside borne to the hospital,
The meeting of enemies, the sudden oath,
    the blows and fall,

The excited crowd, the policeman with
    his star quickly working his passage
    to the centre of the crowd,
The impassive stones that receive and
    return so many echoes,
What groans of over-fed or half-starv'd
    who fall sunstruck or in fits,
What exclamations of women taken
    suddenly who hurry home and give
    birth to babes,
What living and buried speech is always
    vibrating here, what howls restrain'd
    by decorum,
Arrests of criminals, slights, adulterous
    offers made, acceptances, rejections
    with convex lips,
I mind them or the show or resonance of
    them — I come and I depart.

IX

The big doors of the country barn stand
    open and ready,
The dried grass of the harvest-time loads
    the slow-drawn wagon,
The clear light plays on the brown gray
    and green intertinged,
The armfuls are pack'd to the sagging mow.

I am there, I help, I came stretch'd atop
    of the load,

I felt its soft jolts, one leg reclined on the
    other,
I jump from the cross-beams and seize
    the clover and timothy,
And roll head over heels and tangle my
    hair full of wisps.

X

Alone far in the wilds and mountains I
    hunt,
Wandering amazed at my own lightness
    and glee,
In the late afternoon choosing a safe spot
    to pass the night,
Kindling a fire and broiling the fresh-
    kill'd game,
Falling asleep on the gather'd leaves with
    my dog and gun by my side.

The Yankee clipper is under her sky-sails,
    she cuts the sparkle and scud,
My eyes settle the land, I bend at her
    prow or shout joyously from the deck.

The boatmen and clam-diggers arose
    early and stopt for me,
I tuck'd my trowser-ends in my boots and
    went and had a good time;
You should have been with us that day
    round the chowder-kettle.

I saw the marriage of the trapper in the
    open air in the far west, the bride was
    a red girl,
Her father and his friends sat near cross-
    legged and dumbly smoking, they had
    moccasins to their feet and large
    thick blankets hanging from their
    shoulders,
On a bank lounged the trapper, he was
    drest mostly in skins, his luxuriant
    beard and curls protected his neck,
    he held his bride by the hand,
She had long eyelashes, her head was
    bare, her coarse straight locks
    descended upon her voluptuous limbs
    and reach'd to her feet.

The runaway slave came to my house and
    stopt outside,
I heard his motions crackling the twigs of
    the woodpile,
Through the swung half-door of the
    kitchen I saw him limpsy and weak,
And went where he sat on a log and led
    him in and assured him,
And brought water and fill'd a tub for his
    sweated body and bruis'd feet,
And gave him a room that enter'd from
    my own, and gave him some coarse
    clean clothes,

And remember perfectly well his revolving
    eyes and his awkwardness,
And remember putting plasters on the
    galls of his neck and ankles;
He staid with me a week before he was
    recuperated and pass'd north,
I had him sit next me at table, my
    fire-lock lean'd in the corner.

XI

Twenty-eight young men bathe by the
    shore,
Twenty-eight young men and all so
    friendly;
Twenty-eight years of womanly life and
    all so lonesome.

She owns the fine house by the rise of the
    bank,
She hides handsome and richly drest aft
    the blinds of the window.

Which of the young men does she like the
    best?
Ah the homeliest of them is beautiful to
    her.

Where are you off to, lady? for I see you,
You splash in the water there, yet stay
    stock still in your room.

Dancing and laughing along the beach
     came the twenty-ninth bather,
The rest did not see her, but she saw
     them and loved them.

The beards of the young men glisten'd
     with wet, it ran from their long hair,
Little streams pass'd all over their
     bodies.

As unseen hand also pass'd over their
     bodies,
It descended tremblingly from their
     temples and ribs.

The young men float on their backs,
     their white bellies bulge to the sun,
     they do not ask who seizes fast to
     them,
They do not know who puffs and declines
     with pendant and bending arch,
They do not think whom they souse with
     spray.

XII

The butcher-boy puts off his
     killing-clothes, or sharpens his knife
     at the stall in the market,
I loiter enjoying his repartee and his
     shuffle and break-down.

Blacksmiths with grimed and hairy chests
environ the anvil,
Each has his main-sledge, they are all out,
there is a great heat in the fire.

From the cinder-strew'd threshold I
follow their movements,
The lithe sheer of their waists plays even
with their massive arms,
Overhand the hammers swing, overhand
so slow, overhand so sure,
They do not hasten, each man hits in his
place.

XIII

The negro holds firmly the reins of his
four horses, the block swags
underneath on its tied-over chain,
The negro that drives the long dray of
the stone-yard, steady and tall he
stands pois'd on one leg on the
string-piece,
His blue shirt exposes his ample neck and
breast and loosens over his hip-band,
His glance is calm and commanding, he
tosses the slouch of his hat away from
his forehead,
The sun falls on his crispy hair and
mustache, falls on the black of his
polish'd and perfect limbs.

I behold the picturesque giant and love
    him, and I do not stop there,
I go with the team also.

In me the caresser of life wherever
    moving, backward as well as forward
    sluing,
To niches aside and junior bending, not a
    person or object missing,
Absorbing all to myself and for this song.

Oxen that rattle the yoke and chain or
    halt in the leafy shade, what is that
    you express in your eyes?
It seems to me more than all the print I
    have read in my life.

My tread scares the wood-drake and
    wood-duck on my distant and
    day-long ramble,
They rise together, they slowly circle
    around.

I believe in those wing'd purposes,
And acknowledge red, yellow, white,
    playing within me,
And consider green and violet and the
    tufted crown intentional,
And do not call the tortoise unworthy
    because she is not something else,

And the jay in the woods never studied
    the gamut, yet trills pretty well to me,
And the look of the bay mare shames
    silliness out of me.

XIV

The wild gander leads his flock through
    the cool night,
Ya-honk he says, and sounds it down to
    me like an invitation,
The pert may suppose it meaningless, but
    I listening close,
Find its purpose and place up there
    toward the wintry sky.

The sharp-hoof'd moose of the north, the
    cat on the house-sill, the chickadee,
    the prairie-dog,
The litter of the grunting sow as they tug
    at her teats,
The brood of the turkey-hen and she with
    her halfspread wings,
I see in them and myself the same old law.

The press of my foot to the earth springs
    a hundred affections,
They scorn the best I can do to relate
    them.

I am enamour'd of growing out-doors,

Of men that live among cattle or taste of
    the ocean or woods,
Of the builders and steerers of
    ships and the wielders of axes
    and mauls, and the drivers of
    horses,
I can eat and sleep with them week in
    and week out.

What is commonest, cheapest, nearest,
    easiest, is Me,
Me going in for my chances, spending for
    vast returns,
Adorning myself to bestow myself on the
    first that will take me,
Not asking the sky to come down to my
    good will,
Scattering it freely forever.

XV

The pure contralto sings in the organ
    loft,
The carpenter dresses his plank, the
    tongue of his foreplane whistles its
    wild ascending lisp,
The married and unmarried children
    ride home to their Thanksgiving
    dinner,
The pilot seizes the king-pin, he heaves
    down with a strong arm,

The mate stands braced in the whale-boat,
    lance and harpoon are ready,
The duck-shooter walks by silent and
    cautious stretches,
The deacons are ordain'd with cross'd
    hands at the altar,
The spinning-girl retreats and advances to
    the hum of the big wheel,
The farmer stops by the bars as he walks
    on a First-day loafe and looks at the
    oats and rye,
The lunatic is carried at last to the
    asylum a confirm'd case,
(He will never sleep any more as he did
    in the cot in his mother's bed-room;)
The jour printer with gray head and
    gaunt jaws works at his case,
He turns his quid of tobacco while his
    eyes blurr with the manuscript;
The malform'd limbs are tied to the
    surgeon's table,
What is removed drops horribly in a pail;
The quadroon girl is sold at the auction-
    stand, the drunkard nods by the bar-
    room stove,
The machinist rolls up his sleeves, the
    policeman travels his beat, the gate-
    keeper marks who pass,
The young fellow drives the express-wagon,
    (I love him, though I do not know him;)

The half-breed straps on his light boots
    to compete in the race,
The western turkey-shooting draws old
    and young, some lean on their rifles,
    some sit on logs,
Out from the crowd steps the marksman,
    takes his position, levels his piece;
The groups of newly-come immigrants
    cover the wharf or levee,
As the wooly-pates hoe in the sugar-field,
    the overseer views them from his
    saddle,
The bugle calls in the ball-room, the
    gentlemen run for their partners, the
    dancers bow to each other,
The youth lies awake in the cedar-roof'd
    garret and harks to the musical rain,
The Wolverine sets traps on the creek
    that helps fill the Huron,
The squaw wrapt in her yellow-hemm'd
    cloth is offering moccasins and
    bead-bags for sale,
The connoisseur peers along the
    exhibition-gallery with half-shut eyes
    bent sideways,
As the deck-hands make fast the
    steamboat the plank is thrown for the
    shore-going passengers,
The young sister holds out the skein
    while the elder sister winds it off in a

ball, and stops now and then for the
  knots,
The one-year wife is recovering and
  happy having a week ago borne her
  first child,
The clean-hair'd Yankee girl works with
  her sewing-machine or in the factory
  or mill,
The paving-man leans on his two-handed
  rammer, the reporter's lead flies
  swiftly over the note-book, the sign-
  painter is lettering with blue and
  gold,
The canal boy trots on the tow-path, the
  book-keeper counts at his desk, the
  shoemaker waxes his thread,
The conductor beats time for the band
  and all the performers follow him,
The child is baptized, the convert is
  making his first professions,
The regatta is spread on the bay, the race
  is begun, (how the white sails sparkle!)
The drover watching his drove sings out
  to them that would stray,
The pedler sweats with his pack on his
  back, (the purchaser higgling about
  the odd cent;)
The bride unrumples her white dress, the
  minute-hand of the clock moves
  slowly,

The opium-eater reclines with rigid head
and justopen'd lips,
The prostitute draggles her shawl, her
bonnet bobs on her tipsy and
pimpled neck,
The crowd laugh at her blackguard
oaths, the men jeer and wink to each
other,
(Miserable! I do not laugh at your oaths
nor jeer you;)
The President holding a cabinet council
is surrounded by the great Secretaries,
On the peazza walk three matrons stately
and friendly with twinied arms,
The crew of the fish-smack pack repeated
layers of halibut in the hold,
The Missourian crosses the plains toting
his wares and his cattle,
As the fare-collector goes through the
train he gives notice by the jingling of
loose change,
The floor-men are laying the floor, the
tinners are tinning the roof, the
masons are calling for mortar,
In single file each shouldering his hod
pass onward the laborers;
Seasons pursuing each other the
indescribable crowd is gather'd, it is
the fourth of Seventh-month, (what
salutes of cannon and small arms!)

Seasons pursuing each other the plougher
   ploughs, the mower mows, and the
   winter-grain falls in the ground;
Off on the lakes the pike-fisher watches
   and waits by the hole in the frozen
   surface,
The stumps stand thick round the
   clearing, the squatter strikes deep
   with his axe,
Flatboatmen make fast towards dusk near
   the cottonwood or pecan-trees,
Coon-seekers go through the regions of
   the Red river or through those
   drain'd by the Tennessee, or through
   those of the Arkansas,
Torches shine in the dark that hangs on
   the Chattahooche or Altamahaw,
Patriarchs sit at supper with sons and
   grandsons and great-grandsons
   around them,
In walls of adobie, in canvas tents, rest
   hunters and trappers after their day's
   sport,
The city sleeps and the country sleeps,
The living sleep for their time, the dead
   sleep for their time,
The old husband sleeps by his wife and
   the young husband sleeps by his wife;
And these tend inward to me, and I tend
   outward to them,

And such as it is to be of these more or
    less I am,
And of these one and all I weave the song
    of myself.

XVI

I am of old and young, of the foolish as
    much as the wise,
Regardless of others, ever regardful of
    others,
Maternal as well as paternal, a child as
    well as a man,
Stuff'd with the stuff that is coarse and
    stuff'd with the stuff that is fine,

One of the Nation of many nations, the
    smallest the same and the largest the
    same,
A Southerner soon as a Northerner, a
    planter nonchalant and hospitable
    down by the Oconee I live,
A Yankee bound my own way ready for
    trade, my joints the limberest joints
    on earth and the sternest joints on
    earth,
A Kentuckian walking the vale of the
    Elkhorn in my deer-skin leggings, a
    Louisianian or Georgian,
A boatman over lakes or bays or along
    coasts, a Hoosier, Badger, Buckeye;

At home on Kanadian snow-slopes or up
in the bush, or with fishermen off
Newfoundland,
At home in the fleet of ice-boats, sailing
with the rest and tacking,
At home on the hills of Vermont or in
the woods of Maine, or the Texan
ranch,
Comrade of Californians, comrade of free
North-Westerners, (loving their big
proportions,)
Comrade of raftsmen and coalmen,
comrade of all who shake hands and
welcome to drink and meat,
A learner with the simplest, a teacher of
the thoughtfullest,
A novice beginning yet experient of
myriads of seasons,
Of every hue and caste am I, of every
rank and religion,
A farmer, mechanic, artist, gentleman,
sailor, quaker,
Prisoner, fancy-man, rowdy, lawyer,
physician, priest.

I resist any thing better than my own
diversity,
Breathe the air but leave plenty after me,
And am not stuck up, and am in my
place.

(The moth and the fish-eggs are in their
   place,
The bright suns I see and the dark suns I
   cannot see are in their place,
The palpable is in its place and the
   impalpable is in its place.)

XVII

These are really the thoughts of all men
   in all ages and lands, they are not
   original with me,
If they are not yours as much as mine
   they are nothing, or next to
   nothing,
If they are not the riddle and the untying
   of the riddle they are nothing,
If they are not just as close as they are
   distant they are nothing.

This is the grass that grows wherever the
   land is and the water is,
This the common air that bathes the
   globe.

XVIII

With music strong I come, with my
   cornets and my drums,
I play not marches for accepted victors
   only, I play marches for conquer'd
   and slain persons.

Have you heard that it was good to gain
 the day?
I also say it is good to fall, battles are lost
 in the same spirit in which they are
 won.

I beat and pound for the dead,
I blow through my embouchures my
 loudest and gayest for them.

Vivas to those who have fail'd!
And to those whose war-vessels sank in
 the sea!
And to those themselves who sank in the
 sea!
And to the generals that lost
 engagements, and all overcome
 heroes!
And the numberless unknown heroes
 equal to the greatest heroes known!

XIX

This is the meal equally set, this the meat
 for natural hunger,
It is for the wicked just the same as the
 righteous, I make appointments with
 all,

I will not have a single person slighted or
 left away,

The kept-woman, sponger, thief, are
     hereby invited,
The heavy-lipp'd slave is invited, the
     venerealee is invited;
There shall be no difference between
     them and the rest.

This is the press of a bashful hand, this
     the float and odor of hair,
This the touch of my lips to yours, this
     the murmur of yearning,
This the far-off depth and height
     reflecting my own face,
This the thoughtful merge of myself, and
     the outlet again.

Do you guess I have some intricate purpose?
Well I have, for the Fourth-month
     showers have, and the mica on the
     side of a rock has.

Do you take it I would astonish?
Does the daylight astonish? does the early
     redstart twittering through the
     woods?
Do I astonish more than they?

This hour I tell things in confidence,
I might not tell everybody, but I will tell
     you.

XX

Who goes there? hankering, gross,
    mystical, nude;
How is it I extract strength from the beef
    I eat?

What is a man anyhow? what am I? what
    are you?

All I mark as my own you shall offset it
    with your own,
Else it were time lost listening to me.

I do not snivel that snivel the world over,
That months are vacuums and the
    ground but wallow and filth.

Whimpering and truckling fold with
    powders for invalids, conformity, goes
    to the fourth-remov'd,
I wear my hat as I please indoors or out.

Why should I pray? why should I venerate
    and be ceremonious?

Having pried through the strata, analyzed
    to a hair, counsel'd with doctors and
    calculated close,
I find no sweeter fat than sticks to my
    own bones.

In all people I see myself, none more and
    not one a barley-corn less,
And the good or bad I say of myself I say
    of them.

I know I am solid and sound,
To me the converging objects of the
    universe perpetually flow,
All are written to me, and I must get
    what the writing means.
I know I am deathless,
I know this orbit of mine cannot be swept
    by a carpenter's compass,
I know I shall not pass like a child's
    carlacue cut with a burnt stick at
    night.

I know I am august,
I do not trouble my spirit to vindicate
    itself or be understood,
I see that the elementary laws never
    apologize,
(I reckon I behave no prouder than the
    level I plant my house by, after all.)

I exist as I am, that is enough,
If no other in the world be aware I sit
    content,
And if each and all be aware I sit
    content.

One world is aware and by far the largest
    to me, and that is myself,
And whether I come to my own to-day or
    in ten thousand or ten million years,
I can cheerfully take it now, or with equal
    cheerfulness I can wait.

My foothold is tenon'd and mortis'd in
    granite,
I laugh at what you call dissolution,
And I know the amplitude of time.

XXI

I am the poet of the Body and I am the
    poet of the Soul,
The pleasures of heaven are with me and
    the pains of hell are with me,
The first I graft and increase upon myself,
    the latter I translate into a new tongue.

I am the poet of the woman the same as
    the man,
And I say it is as great to be a woman as
    to be a man,
And I say there is nothing greater than
    the mother of men.

I chant the chant of dilation or pride,
We have had ducking and deprecating
    about enough,

I show that size is only development.

Have you outstript the rest? are you the
    President?
It is a trifle, they will more than arrive
    there every one, and still pass on.

I am he that walks with the tender and
    growing night,
I call to the earth and sea half-held by
    the night.

Press close bare-bosom'd night — press
    close magnetic nourishing night!
Night of south winds — night of the large
    few stars!
Still nodding night — mad naked summer
    night.

Smile O voluptuous cool-breath'd earth!
Earth of the slumbering and liquid
    trees!
Earth of departed sunset — earth of the
    mountains misty-topt!
Earth of the vitreous pour of the full
    moon just tinged with blue!
Earth of shine and dark mottling the tide
    of the river!
Earth of the limpid gray of clouds
    brighter and clearer for my sake!

Far-swooping elbow'd earth — rich
 apple-blossom'd earth!
Smile, for your lover comes.

Prodigal, you have given me love —
 therefore I to you give love!
O unspeakable passionate love.

XXII

You sea! I resign myself to you also — I
 guess what you mean,
I behold from the beach your crooked
 inviting fingers,
I believe you refuse to go back without
 feeling of me,
We must have a turn together, I undress,
 hurry me out of sight of the land,
Cushion me soft, rock me in billowy
 drowse,
Dash me with amorous wet, I can repay
 you.

Sea of stretch'd ground-swells,
Sea breathing broad and convulsive breaths,
Sea of the brine of life and of unshovell'd
 yet always-ready graves,
Howler and scooper of storms, capricious
 and dainty sea,
I am integral with you, I too am of one
 phase and of all phases.

Partaker of influx and efflux I, extoller of
    hate and conciliation,
Extoller of amies and those that sleep in
    each others' arms.

I am he attesting sympathy,
(Shall I make my list of things in the
    house and skip the house that
    supports them?)

I am not the poet of goodness only, I do
    not decline to be the poet of
    wickedness also.

What blurt is this about virtue and about
    vice?
Evil propels me and reform of evil
    propels me, I stand indifferent,
My gait is no fault-finder's or rejecter's
    gait,
I moisten the roots of all that has
    grown.

Did you fear some scrofula out of the
    unflagging pregnancy?
Did you guess the celestial laws are yet to
    be work'd over and rectified?

I find one side a balance and the
    antipodal side a balance,

Soft doctrine as steady help as stable
  doctrine,
Thoughts and deeds of the present our
  rouse and early start.

This minute that comes to me over the
  past decillions,
There is no better than it and now.

What behaved well in the past or behaves
  well to-day is not such a wonder,
The wonder is always and always how there
  can be a mean man or an infidel.

XXIII

Endless unfolding of words of ages!
And mine a word of the modern, the
  word En-Masse.

A word of the faith that never balks,
Here or henceforward it is all the same to
  me, I accept Time absolutely.

It alone is without flaw, it alone rounds
  and completes all,
That mystic baffling wonder alone
  completes all.

I accept Reality and dare not question it,
Materialism first and last imbuing.

Hurrah for positive science! long live
    exact demonstration!
Fetch stonecrop mixt with cedar and
    branches of lilac,
This is the lexicographer, this the
    chemist, this made a grammar of the
    old cartouches,
These mariners put the ship through
    dangerous unknown seas,
This is the geologist, this works with the
    scalpel, and this is a mathematician.

Gentlemen, to you the first honors
    always!
Your facts are useful, and yet they are not
    my dwelling,
I but enter by them to an area of my
    dwelling.

Less the reminders of properties told my
    words,
And more the reminders they of life
    untold, and of freedom and
    extrication,
And make short account of neuters and
    geldings, and favor men and women
    fully equipt,
And beat the gong of revolt, and stop
    with fugitives and them that plot and
    conspire.

XXIV

Walt Whitman, a kosmos, of Manhattan
    the son,
Turbulent, fleshy, sensual, eating, drinking
    and breeding,
No sentimentalist, no stander above men
    and women or apart from them,
No more modest than immodest.

Unscrew the locks from the doors!
Unscrew the doors themselves from their
    jambs!

Whoever degrades another degrades me,
And whatever is done or said returns at
    last to me.

Through me the afflatus surging and
    surging, through me the current and
    index.

I speak the pass-word primeval, I give the
    sign of democracy,
By God! I will accept nothing which all
    cannot have their counterpart of on
    the same terms.

Through me many long dumb voices,
Voices of the interminable generations of
    prisoners and slaves,

Voices of the diseas'd and despairing and
of thieves and dwarfs,
Voices of cycles of preparation and
accretion,
And of the threads that connect the stars,
and of wombs and of the father-stuff,
And of the rights of them the others are
down upon,
Of the deform'd, trivial, flat, foolish,
despised,
Fog in the air, beetles rolling balls of
dung.

Through me forbidden voices,
Voices of sexes and lusts, voices veil'd and
I remove the veil,
Voices indecent by me clarified and
transfigur'd.

I do not press my fingers across my
mouth,
I keep as delicate around the bowels as
around the head and heart,
Copulation is no more rank to me than
death is.

I believe in the flesh and the appetites,
Seeing, hearing, feeling, are miracles,
and each part and tag of me is a
miracle.

Divine am I inside and out, and I make
      holy whatever I touch or am touch'd
      from,
The scent of these arm-pits aroma finer
      than prayer,
This head more than churches, bibles,
      and all the creeds.

If I worship one thing more than another
      it shall be the spread of my own
      body, or any part of it,
Translucent mould of me it shall be you!
Shaded ledges and rests it shall be you!
Firm masculine colter it shall be you!
Whatever goes to the tilth of me it shall
      be you!
You my rich blood! your milky stream
      pale strippings of my life!
Breast that presses against other breasts it
      shall be you!
My brain it shall be your occult
      convolutions!

Root of wash'd sweet-flag! timorous
      pond-snipe! nest of guarded duplicate
      eggs! it shall be you!
Mix'd tussled hay of head, beard, brawn,
      it shall be you!
Trickling sap of maple, fibre of manly
      wheat, it shall be you!

Sun so generous it shall be you!
Vapors lighting and shading my face it
    shall be you!
You sweaty brooks and dews it shall be
    you!
Winds whose soft-tickling genitals rub
    against me it shall be you!
Broad muscular fields, branches of live
    oak, loving lounger in my winding
    paths, it shall be you!
Hands I have taken, face I have kiss'd,
    mortal I have ever touch'd, it shall be
    you.

I dote on myself, there is a lot of me and
    all so luscious,
Each moment and whatever happens
    thrills me with joy,
I cannot tell how my ankles bend, nor
    whence the cause of my faintest
    wish,
Nor the cause of the friendship I emit,
    nor the cause of the friendship I take
    again.

That I walk up my stoop, I pause to
    consider if it really be,
A morning-glory at my window satisfies
    me more than the metaphysics of
    books.

To behold the day-break!
The little light fades the immense and
   diaphanous shadows,
The air tastes good to my palate.

Hefts of the moving world at innocent
   gambols silently rising freshly exuding,
Scooting obliquely high and low.

Something I cannot see puts upward
   libidinous prongs,
Seas of bright juice suffuse heaven.

The earth by the sky staid with, the daily
   close of their junction,
The heav'd challenge from the east that
   moment over my head,
The mocking taunt, See then whether you
   shall be master!

XXV

Dazzling and tremendous how quick the
   sun-rise would kill me,
If I could not now and always send sun-
   rise out of me.

We also ascend dazzling and tremendous
   as the sun,
We found our own O my soul in the calm
   and cool of the daybreak.

My voice goes after what my eyes cannot
   reach,
With the twirl of my tongue I encompass
   worlds and volumes of worlds.

Speech is the twin of my vision, it is
   unequal to measure itself,
It provokes me forever, it says
   sarcastically,
*Walt you contain enough, why don't you
let it out then?*

Come now I will not be tantalized, you
   conceive too much of articulation,
Do you not know O speech how the buds
   beneath you are folded?
Waiting in gloom, protected by frost,
The dirt receding before my prophetical
   screams,
I underlying causes to balance them at last,
My knowledge my live parts, it keeping
   tally with the meaning of all things,
Happiness, (which whoever hears me let
   him or her set out in search of this
   day.)

My final merit I refuse you, I refuse
   putting from me what I really am,
Encompass worlds, but never try to
   encompass me,

131

I crowd your sleekest and best by simply
    looking toward you.
Writing and talk do not prove me,
I carry the plenum of proof and every
    thing else in my face,
With the hush of my lips I wholly
    confound the skeptic.

XXVI

Now I will do nothing but listen,
To accrue what I hear into this song, to
    let sounds contribute toward it.

I hear bravuras of birds, bustle of growing
    wheat, gossip of flames, clack of
    sticks cooking my meals,
I hear the sound I love, the sound of the
    human voice,
I hear all sounds running together,
    combined, fused or following,
Sounds of the city and sounds out of the
    city, sounds of the day and night,
Talkative young ones to those that like
    them, the loud laugh of work-people
    at their meals,
The angry base of disjointed friendship,
    the faint tones of the sick,
The judge with hands tight to the desk,
    his pallid lips pronouncing a
    death-sentence,

The heave'e'yo of stevedores unlading
   ships by the wharves, the refrain of
   the anchor-lifters,
The ring of alarm-bells, the cry of fire,
   the whirr of swift-streaking engines
   and hose-carts with premonitory
   tinkles and color'd lights,
The steam-whistle, the solid roll of the
   train of approaching cars,
The slow march play'd at the head of
   the association marching two and
   two,
(They go to guard some corpse, the
   flag-tops are draped with black
   muslin.)

I hear the violoncello, ('tis the young
   man's heart's complaint,)
I hear the key'd cornet, it glides quickly
   in through my ears,
It shakes mad-sweet pangs through my
   belly and breast.

I hear the chorus, it is a grand opera,
Ah this indeed is music — this suits me.

A tenor large and fresh as the creation
   fills me,
The orbic flex of his mouth is pouring
   and filling me full.

I hear the train'd soprano (what work
with hers is this?)
The orchestra whirls me wider than
Uranus flies,
It wrenches such ardors from me I did
not know I possess'd them,
It sails me, I dab with bare feet, they are
lick'd by the indolent waves,
I am cut by bitter and angry hail, I lose
my breath,
Steep'd amid honey'd morphine,
my windpipe throttled in fakes of
death,
At length let up again to feel the puzzle
of puzzles,
And that we call Being.

XXVII

To be in any form, what is that?
(Round and round we go, all of us, and
ever come back thither,)
If nothing lay more develop'd the
quahaug in its callous shell were
enough.

Mine is no callous shell,
I have instant conductors all over me
whether I pass or stop,
They seize every object and lead it
harmlessly through me.

I merely stir, press, feel with my fingers,
 and am happy,
To touch my person to some one else's is
 about as much as I can stand.

XXVIII

Is this then a touch? quivering me to a
 new identity,
Flames and ether making a rush for my
 veins,
Treacherous tip of me reaching and
 crowding to help them,
My flesh and blood playing out lightning
 to strike what is hardly different from
 myself,
On all sides prurient provokers stiffening
 my limbs,
Straining the udder of my heart for its
 withheld drip,
Behaving licentious toward me, taking no
 denial,
Depriving me of my best as for a
 purpose,
Unbuttoning my clothes, holding me by
 the bare waist,
Deluding my confusion with the calm of
 the sunlight and pasture-fields,
Immodestly sliding the fellow-senses away,
They bribed to swap off with touch and
 go and graze at the edges of me,

No consideration, no regard for my
    draining strength or my anger,
Fetching the rest of the herd around to
    enjoy them a while,
Then all uniting to stand on a headland
    and worry me.

The sentries desert every other part of me,
They have left me helpless to a red
    marauder,
They all come to the headland to witness
    and assist against me.
I am given up by traitors,
I talk wildly, I have lost my wits, I and
    nobody else am the greatest traitor,
I went myself first to the headland, my
    own hands carried me there.

You villain touch! what are you doing? my
    breath is tight in its throat,
Unclench your floodgates, you are too
    much for me.

XXIX
Blind loving wrestling touch, sheath'd
    hooded sharp-tooth'd touch!
Did it make you ache so, leaving me?

Parting track'd by arriving, perpetual
    payment of perpetual loan,

Rich showering rain, and recompense
  richer afterward.

Sprouts take and accumulate, stand by
  the curb prolific and vital,
Landscapes projected masculine,
  full-sized and golden.

XXX

All truths wait in all things,
They neither hasten their own delivery
  nor resist it,
They do not need the obstetric forceps of
  the surgeon,
The insignificant is as big to me as any,
(What is less or more than a touch?)

Logic and sermons never convince,
The damp of the night drives deeper into
  my soul.

(Only what proves itself to every man and
  woman is so,
Only what nobody denies is so.)

A minute and a drop of me settle my brain,
I believe the soggy clods shall become
  lovers and lamps,
And a compend of compends is the meat
  of a man or woman,

And a summit and flower there is the
feeling they have for each other,
And they are to branch boundlessly out
of that lesson until it becomes
omnific,
And until one and all shall delight us,
and we them.

XXXI

I believe a leaf of grass is no less than the
journeywork of the stars,
And the pismire is equally perfect, and a
grain of sand, and the egg of the
wren,
And the tree-toad is a chef-d'œuvre for
the highest,
And the running blackberry would adorn
the parlors of heaven,
And the narrowest hinge in my hand puts
to scorn all machinery,
And the cow crunching with depress'd
head surpasses any statue,
And a mouse is miracle enough to stagger
sextillions of infidels.

I find I incorporate gneiss, coal,
long-threaded moss, fruits, grains,
esculent roots,
And am stucco'd with quadrupeds and
birds all over,

And have distanced what is behind me for
   good reasons,
But call any thing back again when I
   desire it.

In vain the speeding or shyness,
In vain the plutonic-rocks send their old
   heat against my approach,
In vain the mastodon retreats beneath its
   own powder'd bones,
In vain objects stand leagues off and
   assume manifold shapes,
In vain the ocean settling in hollows and
   the great monsters lying low,
In vain the buzzard houses herself with
   the sky,
In vain the snake slides through the
   creepers and logs,
In vain the elk takes to the inner passes
   of the woods,
In vain the razor-bill'd auk sails far north
   to Labrador,
I follow quickly, I ascend to the nest in
   the fissure of the cliff.

XXXII

I think I could turn and live with
   animals, they are so placid and
   self-contain'd,
I stand and look at them long and long.

They do not sweat and whine about their
    condition,
They do not lie awake in the dark and
    weep for their sins,
They do not make me sick discussing
    their duty to God,
Not one is dissatisfied, not one is
    demented with the mania of owning
    things,
Not one kneels to another, nor to his
    kind that lived thousands of years
    ago,
Not one is respectable or unhappy over
    the whole earth.

So they show their relations to me and I
    accept them,
They bring me tokens of myself, they
    evince them plainly in their possession.

I wonder where they get those tokens,
Did I pass that way huge times ago and
    negligently drop them?

Myself moving forward then and now and
    forever,
Gathering and showing more always and
    with velocity,
Infinite and omnigenous, and the like of
    these among them,

Not too exclusive toward the reachers of
    my remembrancers,
Picking out here one that I love, and now
    go with him on brotherly terms.

A gigantic beauty of a stallion, fresh and
    responsive to my caresses,
Head high in the forehead, wide between
    the ears,
Limbs glossy and supple, tail dusting the
    ground,
Eyes full of sparkling wickedness, ears
    finely cut, flexibly moving.

His nostrils dilate as my heels embrace
    him,
His well-built limbs tremble with pleasure
    as we race around and return.

I but use you a minute, then I resign you,
    stallion,
Why do I need your paces when I myself
    out-gallop them?
Even as I stand or sit passing faster than
    you.

XXXIII

Space and Time! now I see it is true,
    what I guess'd at,
What I guess'd when I loaf'd on the grass,

141

What I guess'd while I lay alone in my
    bed,
And again as I walk'd the beach under
    the paling stars of the morning.

My ties and ballasts leave me, my elbows
    rest in sea-gaps,
I skirt sierras, my palms cover continents,
I am afoot with my vision.

By the city's quadrangular houses — in
    log huts, camping with lumbermen,
Along the ruts of the turnpike, along the
    dry gulch and rivulet bed,
Weeding my onion-patch or hoeing rows
    of carrots and parsnips, crossing
    savannas, trailing in forests,
Prospecting, gold-digging, girdling the
    trees of a new purchase,
Scorch'd ankle-deep by the hot sand,
    hauling by boat down the shallow
    river,
Where the panther walks to and fro on a
    limb overhead, where the buck turns
    furiously at the hunter,
Where the rattlesnake suns his flabby
    length on a rock, where the otter is
    feeding on fish,
Where the alligator in his tough pimples
    sleeps by the bayou,

Where the black bear is searching for
roots or honey, where the beaver pats
the mud with his paddle-shaped tail;
Over the growing sugar, over the
yellow-flower'd cotton plant, over the
rice in its low moist field,
Over the sharp-peak'd farm house, with
its scallop'd scum and slender shoots
from the gutters,
Over the western persimmon, over the
long-leav'd corn, over the delicate
blue-flower flax,
Over the white and brown buckwheat, a
hummer and buzzer there with the
rest,
Over the dusky green of the rye as it
ripples and shades in the breeze;
Scaling mountains, pulling myself
cautiously up, holding on by low
scragged limbs,
Walking the path worn in the grass and
beat through the leaves of the
brush,
Where the quail is whistling betwixt the
woods and the wheat-lot,
Where the bat flies in the Seventh-month
eve, where the great goldbug drops
through the dark,
Where the brook puts out of the roots of
the old tree and flows to the meadow,

Where cattle stand and shake away flies
  with the tremulous shuddering of
  their hides,
Where the cheese-cloth hangs in the
  kitchen, where andirons straddle the
  hearth-slab, where cobwebs fall in
  festoons from the rafters;
Where trip-hammers crash, where the
  press is whirling its cylinders,
Wherever the human heart beats with
  terrible throes under its ribs,
Where the pear-shaped balloon is floating
  aloft, (floating in it myself and
  looking composedly down,)
Where the life-car is drawn on the
  slip-noose, where the heat hatches
  pale-green eggs in the dented sand,
Where the she-whale swims with her calf
  and never forsakes it,
Where the steam-ship trails hind-ways its
  long pennant of smoke,
Where the fin of the shark cuts like a
  black chip out of the water,
Where the half-burn'd brig is riding on
  unknown currents,
Where shells grow to her slimy deck,
  where the dead are corrupting
  below;
Where the dense-starr'd flag is borne at
  the head of the regiments,

Approaching Manhattan up by the
    long-stretching island,
Under Niagara, the cataract falling like a
    veil over my countenance,
Upon a door-step, upon the horse-block
    of hard wood outside,
Upon the race-course, or enjoying
    picnics or jigs or a good game of
    baseball,
At he-festivals, with blackguard gibes,
    ironical license, bull-dances, drinking,
    laughter,
At the cider-mill tasting the sweets of the
    brown mash, sucking the juice
    through a straw,
At apple-peelings wanting kisses for all
    the red fruit I find,
At musters, beach-parties, friendly bees,
    huskings, house-raisings;
Where the mocking-bird sounds his
    delicious gurgles, cackles, screams,
    weeps,
Where the hay-rick stands in the
    barn-yard, where the dry-stalks are
    scatter'd, where the brood-cow waits
    in the hovel,
Where the bull advances to do his
    masculine work, where the stud to
    the mare, where the cock is treading
    the hen,

Where the heifers browse, where geese
    nip their food with short jerks,
Where sun-down shadows lengthen over
    the limitless and lonesome prairie,
Where herds of buffalo make a crawling
    spread of the square miles far and
    near,
Where the humming-bird shimmers,
    where the neck of the long-lived swan
    is curving and winding,
Where the laughing-gull scoots by the
    shore, where she laughs her
    near-human laugh,
Where bee-hives range on a gray bench in
    the garden half hid by the high
    weeds,
Where band-neck'd partridges roost in a
    ring on the ground with their heads
    out,
Where burial coaches enter the arch'd
    gates of a cemetery,
Where winter wolves bark amid wastes of
    snow and icicled trees,
Where the yellow-crown'd heron comes to
    the edge of the marsh at night and
    feeds upon small crabs,
Where the splash of swimmers and divers
    cools the warm noon,
Where the katy-did works her chromatic
    reed on the walnut-tree over the well,

Through patches of citrons and
  cucumbers with silver-wired leaves,
Through the salt-lick or orange glade, or
  under conical firs,
Through the gymnasium, through the
  curtain'd saloon, through the office or
  public hall;
Pleas'd with the native and pleas'd with
  the foreign, pleas'd with the new and
  old,
Pleas'd with the homely woman as well as
  the handsome,
Pleas'd with the quakeress as she puts off
  her bonnet and talks melodiously,
Pleas'd with the tune of the choir of the
  whitewash'd church,
Pleas'd with the earnest words of the
  sweating Methodist preacher,
  impress'd seriously at the
  camp-meeting;
Looking in at the shop windows of
  Broadway the whole forenoon, flatting
  the flesh of my nose on the thick
  plate glass,
Wandering the same afternoon with my
  face turn'd up to the clouds, or down
  a lane or along the beach,
My right and left arms round the
  sides of two friends, and I in the
  middle;

Coming home with the silent and
    dark-cheek'd bushboy, (behind me he
    rides at the drape of the day,)
Far from the settlements studying the
    print of animals' feet, or the moccasin
    print,
By the cot in the hospital reaching
    lemonade to a feverish patient,
Nigh the coffin'd corpse when all is still,
    examining with a candle;
Voyaging to every port to dicker and
    adventure,
Hurrying with the modern crowd as eager
    and fickle as any,
Hot toward one I hate, ready in my
    madness to knife him,
Solitary at midnight in my back yard,
    my thoughts gone from me a long
    while,
Walking the old hills of Judaea with the
    beautiful gentle God by my side,
Speeding through space, speeding
    through heaven and the stars,
Speeding amid the seven satellites and the
    broad ring, and the diameter of
    eighty thousand miles,
Speeding with tail'd meteors, throwing
    fire-balls like the rest,
Carrying the crescent child that carries its
    own full mother in its belly,

148

Storming, enjoying, planning, loving,
    cautioning,
Backing and filling, appearing and
    disappearing,
I tread day and night such roads.
I visit the orchards of spheres and look at
    the product,
And look at quintillions ripen'd and look
    at quintillions green.

I fly those flights of a fluid and
    swallowing soul,
My course runs below the soundings of
    plummets.

I help myself to material and immaterial,
No guard can shut me off, no law prevent
    me.

I anchor my ship for a little while only,
My messengers continually cruise away or
    bring their returns to me.

I go hunting polar furs and the seal, leaping
    chasms with a pike-pointed staff,
    clinging to topples of brittle and blue.

I ascend to the foretruck,
I take my place late at night in the
    crow's-nest,

We sail the arctic sea, it is plenty light
    enough,
Through the clear atmosphere I stretch
    around on the wonderful beauty,
The enormous masses of ice pass me and
    I pass them, the scenery is plain in all
    directions,
The white-topt mountains show in the
    distance, I fling out my fancies
    toward them,

We are approaching some great
    battle-field in which we are soon to
    be engaged,
We pass the colossal outposts of the
    encampment, we pass with still feet
    and caution,
Or we are entering by the suburbs some
    vast and ruin'd city,
The blocks and fallen architecture more
    than all the living cities of the globe.

I am a free companion, I bivouac by
    invading watchfires,
I turn the bridegroom out of bed and
    stay with the bride myself,
I tighten her all night to my thighs and lips.

My voice is the wife's voice, the screech
    by the rail of the stairs,

They fetch my man's body up dripping
and drown'd.

I understand the large hearts of heroes,
The courage of present times and all
times,
How the skipper saw the crowded and
rudderless wreck of the steam-ship,
and Death chasing it up and down
the storm,
How he knuckled tight and gave not back
an inch, and was faithful of days and
faithful of nights,
And chalk'd in large letters on a board,
*Be of good cheer, we will not desert
you;*
How he follow'd with them and tack'd
with them three days and would not
give it up,
How he saved the drifting company at
last,
How the lank loose-gown'd women look'd
when boated from the side of their
prepared graves,
How the silent old-faced infants and the
lifted sick, and the sharp-lipp'd
unshaved men;
All this I swallow, it tastes good, I like it
well, it becomes mine,
I am the man, I suffer'd, I was there.

The disdain and calmness of martyrs,
The mother of old, condemn'd for a
    witch, burnt with dry wood, her
    children gazing on,
The hounded slave that flags in the race,
    leans by the fence, blowing, cover'd
    with sweat,
The twinges that sting like needles his
    legs and neck, the murderous
    buckshot and the bullets,
All these I feel or am.

I am the hounded slave, I wince at the
    bite of the dogs,
Hell and despair are upon me, crack and
    again crack the marksmen,
I clutch the rails of the fence, my gore
    dribs, thinn'd with the ooze of my
    skin,

I fall on the weeds and stones,
The riders spur their unwilling horses,
    haul close,
Taunt my dizzy ears and beat me violently
    over the head with whip-stocks.

Agonies are one of my changes of garments,
I do not ask the wounded person how he
    feels, I myself become the wounded
    person,

My hurts turn livid upon me as I lean on
    a cane and observe.

I am the mash'd fireman with breast-bone
    broken,
Tumbling walls buried me in their debris,
Heat and smoke I inspired, I heard the
    yelling shouts of my comrades,
I heard the distant click of their picks and
    shovels,
They have clear'd the beams away, they
    tenderly lift me forth.

I lie in the night air in my red shirt, the
    pervading hush is for my sake,
Painless after all I lie exhausted but not
    so unhappy,
White and beautiful are the faces around
    me, the heads are bared of their
    fire-caps,
The kneeling crowd fades with the light
    of the torches.

Distant and dead resuscitate,
They show as the dial or move as the
    hands of me, I am the clock myself.

I am an old artillerist, I tell of my fort's
    bombardment,
I am there again.

Again the long roll of the drummers,
Again the attacking cannon, mortars,
Again to my listening ears the cannon
    responsive.

I take part, I see and hear the whole,
The cries, curses, roar, the plaudits for
    well-aim'd shots,
The ambulanza slowly passing trailing its
    red drip,
Workingmen searching after damages,
    making indispensable repairs,
The fall of grenades through the rent
    roof, the fan-shaped explosion,
The whizz of limbs, heads, stone, wood,
    iron, high in the air.

Again gurgles the mouth of my dying
    general, he furiously waves with his
    hand,
He gasps through the clot *Mind not me*
    — mind — the entrenchments.

XXXIV

Now I tell what I knew in Texas in my
    early youth,
(I tell not the fall of Alamo,
Not one escaped to tell the fall of Alamo,
The hundred and fifty are dumb yet at
    Alamo,)

'Tis the tale of the murder in cold blood
 of four hundred and twelve young
 men.

Retreating they had form'd in a hollow
 square with their baggage for
 breastworks,
Nine hundred lives out of the
 surrounding enemy's, nine times their
 number, was the price they took in
 advance,
Their colonel was wounded and their
 ammunition gone,
They treated for an honorable
 capitulation, receiv'd writing and seal,
 gave up their arms and march'd back
 prisoners of war.

They were the glory of the race of rangers,
Matchless with horse, rifle, song, supper,
 courtship,
Large, turbulent, generous, handsome,
 proud, and affectionate,
Bearded, sunburnt, drest in the free
 costume of hunters,
Not a single one over thirty years of age.

The second First-day morning they were
 brought out in squads and massacred,
 it was beautiful early summer,

The work commenced about five o'clock
    and was over by eight.

None obey'd the command to kneel,
Some made a mad and helpless rush,
    some stood stark and straight,
A few fell at once, shot in the temple or
    heart, the living and dead lay
    together,
The maim'd and mangled dug in the dirt,
    the newcomers saw them there,
Some half-kill'd attempted to crawl
    away,
These were despatch'd with bayonets or
    batter'd with the blunts of muskets,
A youth not seventeen years old seiz'd his
    assassin till two more came to release
    him,
The three were all torn and cover'd with
    the boy's blood.

At eleven o'clock began the burning of
    the bodies;
That is the tale of the murder of the four
    hundred and twelve young men.

XXXV
Would you hear of an old-time sea-fight?
Would you learn who won by the light of
    the moon and stars?

List to the yarn, as my grandmother's
    father the sailor told it to me.

Our foe was no skulk in his ship I tell
    you, (said he,)
His was the surly English pluck, and
    there is no tougher or truer, and
    never was, and never will be;
Along the lower'd eve he came horribly
    raking us.

We closed with him, the yards entangled,
    the cannon touch'd,
My captain lash'd fast with his own
    hands.

We had receiv'd some eighteen pound
    shots under the water,
On our lower-gun-deck two large
    pieces had burst at the first fire,
    killing all around and blowing up
    overhead.

Fighting at sun-down, fighting at dark,
Ten o'clock at night, the full moon well
    up, our leaks on the gain, and five
    feet of water reported,
The master-at-arms loosing the prisoners
    confined in the after-hold to give
    them a chance for themselves.

The transit to and from the magazine is
    now stopt by the sentinels,
They see so many strange faces they do
    not know whom to trust.

Our frigate takes fire,
The other asks if we demand quarter?
If our colors are struck and the fighting
    done?

Now I laugh content, for I hear the voice
    of my little captain,
We have not struck, he composedly cries,
    *we have just begun our part of the
    fighting.*

Only three guns are in use,
One is directed by the captain himself
    against the enemy's mainmast,
Two well serv'd with grape and canister
    silence his musketry and clear his
    decks.

The tops alone second the fire of this
    little battery, especially the main-top,
They hold out bravely during the whole
    of the action.
Not a moment's cease,
The leaks gain fast on the pumps, the fire
    eats toward the powder-magazine.

One of the pumps has been shot
    away, it is generally thought we are
    sinking.

Serene stands the little captain,
He is not hurried, his voice is neither
    high nor low,
His eyes give more light to us than our
    battle-lanterns.

Toward twelve there in the beams of the
    moon they surrender to us.

XXXVI
Stretch'd and still lies the midnight,
Two great hulls motionless on the breast
    of the darkness,
Our vessel riddled and slowly sinking,
    preparations to pass to the one we
    have conquer'd,
The captain on the quarter-deck coldly
    giving his orders through a
    countenance white as a sheet,
Near by the corpse of the child that
    serv'd in the cabin,
The dead face of an old salt with long
    white hair and carefully curl'd
    whiskers,
The flames spite of all that can be done
    flickering aloft and below,

The husky voices of the two or three
    officers yet fit for duty,
Formless stacks of bodies and bodies by
    themselves, dabs of flesh upon the
    masts and spars,
Cut of cordage, dangle of rigging, slight
    shock of the soothe of waves,
Black and impassive guns, litter of
    powder-parcels, strong scent,
A few large stars overhead, silent and
    mournful shining,
Delicate sniffs of sea-breeze, smells of
    sedgy grass and fields by the shore,
    death-messages given in charge to
    survivors,
The hiss of the surgeon's knife, the
    gnawing teeth of his saw,
Wheeze, cluck, swash of falling blood,
    short wild scream, and long, dull,
    tapering groan,
These so, these irretrievable.

XXXVII

You laggards there on guard! look to your
    arms!
In at the conquer'd doors they crowd! I
    am possess'd!
Embody all presences outlaw'd or suffering,
See myself in prison shaped like another
    man,

160

And feel the dull unintermitted pain.

For me the keepers of convicts shoulder
     their carbines and keep watch,
It is I let out in the morning and barr'd
     at night.

Not a mutineer walks handcuff'd to jail
     but I am handcuff'd to him and walk
     by his side,
(I am less the jolly one there, and more
     the silent one with sweat on my
     twitching lips.)

Not a youngster is taken for larceny but I
     go up too, and am tried and
     sentenced.

Not a cholera patient lies at the last gasp
     but I also lie at the last gasp,
My face is ash-color'd, my sinews gnarl,
     away from me people retreat.

Askers embody themselves in me and I
     am embodied in them,
I project my hat, sit shame-faced, and beg.

XXXVIII
Enough! enough! enough!
Somehow I have been stunn'd. Stand back!

Give me a little time beyond my cuff'd
    head, slumbers, dreams, gaping,
I discover myself on the verge of a usual
    mistake.

That I could forget the mockers and
    insults!
That I could forget the trickling tears and
    the blows of the bludgeons and
    hammers!
That I could look with a separate look on
    my own crucifixion and bloody
    crowning.

I remember now,
I resume the overstaid fraction,
The grave of rock multiplies what has
    been confined to it, or to any graves,
Corpses rise, gashes heal, fastenings roll
    from me.

I troop forth replenish'd with supreme
    power, one of an average unending
    procession,
Inland and sea-coast we go, and pass all
    boundary lines,
Our swift ordinances on their way over
    the whole earth,
The blossoms we wear in our hats the
    growth of thousands of years.

Eleves, I salute you! come forward!
Continue your annotations, continue your
  questionings.

XXXIX

The friendly and flowing savage, who is
  he?
Is he waiting for civilization, or past it
  and mastering it?

Is he some Southwesterner rais'd out-doors?
  is he Kanadian?
Is he from the Mississippi country? Iowa,
  Oregon, California?
The mountains? prairie-life, bush-life? or
  sailor from the sea?

Wherever he goes men and women accept
  and desire him,
They desire he should like them,
  touch them, speak to them, stay
  with them.

Behavior lawless as snow-flakes, words
  simple as grass, uncomb'd head,
  laughter, and naiveté,
Slow-stepping feet, common features,
  common modes and emanations,
They descend in new forms from the tips
  of his fingers,

They are wafted with the odor of his
   body or breath, they fly out of the
   glance of his eyes.

XL

Flaunt of the sunshine I need not your
   bask — lie over!
You light surfaces only, I force surfaces
   and depths also.

Earth! you seem to look for something at
   my hands,
Say, old top-knot, what do you want?

Man or woman, I might tell how I like
   you, but cannot,
And might tell what it is in me and what
   it is in you, but cannot,
And might tell that pining I have, that
   pulse of my nights and days.

Behold, I do not give lectures or a little
   charity,
When I give I give myself.

You there, impotent, loose in the knees,
Open your scarf'd chops till I blow grit
   within you,
Spread your palms and lift the flaps of
   your pockets,

I am not to be denied, I compel, I have
        stores plenty and to spare,
And any thing I have I bestow.

I do not ask who you are, that is not
        important to me,
You can do nothing and be nothing but
        what I will infold you.

To cotton-field drudge or cleaner of
        privies I lean,
On his right cheek I put the family kiss,
And in my soul I swear I never will deny
        him.

On women fit for conception I start
        bigger and nimbler babes,
(This day I am jetting the stuff of far
        more arrogant republics.)

To any one dying, thither I speed and
        twist the knob of the door,
Turn the bed-clothes toward the foot of
        the bed,
Let the physician and the priest go
        home.

I seize the descending man and raise him
        with resistless will,
O despairer, here is my neck,

By God, you shall not go down! hang
  your whole weight upon me.

I dilate you with tremendous breath, I
  buoy you up,
Every room of the house do I fill with an
  arm'd force,
Lovers of me, bafflers of graves.

Sleep — I and they keep guard all
  night,
Not doubt, not decease shall dare to lay
  finger upon you,

I have embraced you, and henceforth
  possess you to myself,
And when you rise in the morning you
  will find what I tell you is so.

XLI

I am he bringing help for the sick as they
  pant on their backs,
And for strong upright men I bring yet
  more needed help.

I heard what was said of the universe,
Heard it and heard it of several thousand
  years;
It is middling well as far as it goes — but
  is that all?

Magnifying and applying come I,
Outbidding at the start the old cautious
    hucksters,
Taking myself the exact dimensions of
    Jehovah,
Lithographing Kronos, Zeus his son, and
    Hercules his grandson,
Buying drafts of Osiris, Isis, Belus,
    Brahma, Buddha,
In my portfolio placing Manito loose,
    Allah on a leaf, the crucifix
    engraved,
With Odin and the hideous-faced Mexitli
    and every idol and image,
Taking them all for what they are worth
    and not a cent more,
Admitting they were alive and did the
    work of their days,
(They bore mites as for unfledg'd birds
    who have now to rise and fly and sing
    for themselves,)
Accepting the rough deific sketches
    to fill out better in myself, bestowing
    them freely on each man and woman
    I see,
Discovering as much or more in a framer
    framing a house,
Putting higher claims for him there with
    his roll'd-up sleeves driving the mallet
    and chisel,

167

Not objecting to special revelations,
    considering a curl of smoke or a hair
    on the back of my hand just as
    curious as any revelation,
Lads ahold of fire-engines and
    hook-and-ladder ropes no less to me
    than the gods of the antique wars,
Minding their voices peal through the
    crash of destruction,
Their brawny limbs passing safe over
    charr'd laths, their white foreheads
    whole and unhurt out of the flames;
By the mechanic's wife with her babe at
    her nipple interceding for every
    person born,
Three scythes at harvest whizzing in a
    row from three lusty angels with
    shirts bagg'd out at their waists,
The snag-tooth'd hostler with red hair
    redeeming sins past and to come,
Selling all he possesses, traveling on foot
    to fee lawyers for his brother and sit
    by him while he is tried for forgery;
What was strewn in the amplest strewing
    the square rod about me, and not
    filling the square rod then,
The bull and the bug never worshipp'd
    half enough,
Dung and dirt more admirable than was
    dream'd,

The supernatural of no account, myself
    waiting my time to be one of the
    supremes,
The day getting ready for me when I shall
    do as much good as the best, and be
    as prodigious;
By my life-lumps! becoming already a
    creator,
Putting myself here and now to the
    ambush'd womb of the shadows.

XLII

A call in the midst of the crowd,
My own voice, orotund sweeping and
    final.

Come my children,
Come my boys and girls, my women,
    household and intimates,
Now the performer launches his nerve,
    he has pass'd his prelude on the reeds
    within.

Easily written loose-finger'd chords — I
    feel the thrum of your climax and close.

My head slues round on my neck,
Music rolls, but not from the organ,
Folks are around me, but they are no
    household of mine.

Ever the hard unsunk ground,
Ever the eaters and drinkers, ever the
    upward and downward sun, ever the
    air and the ceaseless tides,
Ever myself and my neighbors, refreshing,
    wicked, real,
Ever the old inexplicable query, ever that
    thorn'd thumb, that breath of itches
    and thirsts,
Ever the vexer's *hoot! hoot!* till we find
    where the sly one hides and bring
    him forth,
Ever love, ever the sobbing liquid
    of life,
Ever the bandage under the chin, ever the
    trestles of death.

Here and there with dimes on the eyes
    walking,
To feed the greed of the belly the brains
    liberally spooning,
Tickets buying, taking, selling, but in to
    the feast never once going,
Many sweating, ploughing, thrashing,
    and then the chaff for payment
    receiving,
A few idly owning, and they the wheat
    continually claiming.
This is the city and I am one of the
    citizens,

Whatever interests the rest interests me,
   politics, wars, markets, newspapers,
   schools,
The mayor and councils, banks, tariffs,
   steamships, factories, stocks, stores,
   real estate and personal estate.

The little plentiful manikins skipping
   around in collars and tail'd coats,
I am aware who they are, (they are
   positively not worms or fleas,)
I acknowledge the duplicates of myself,
   the weakest and shallowest is
   deathless with me,
What I do and say the same waits for
   them,
Every thought that flounders in me the
   same flounders in them.

I know perfectly well my own egotism,
Know my omnivorous lines and must not
   write any less,
And would fetch you whoever you are
   flush with myself.

Not words of routine this song of mine,
But abruptly to question, to leap beyond
   yet nearer bring;
This printed and bound book — but the
   printer and the printing-office boy?

The well-taken photographs — but your
    wife or friend close and solid in your
    arms?
The black ship mail'd with iron, her
    mighty guns in her turrets — but
    the pluck of the captain and
    engineers?
In the houses the dishes and fare and
    furniture — but the host and hostess,
    and the look out of their eyes?
The sky up there — yet here or next
    door, or across the way?
The saints and sages in history — but
    you yourself?
Sermons, creeds, theology — but the
    fathomless human brain,
And what is reason? and what is love?
    and what is life?

XLIII

I do not despise you priests, all time, the
    world over,
My faith is the greatest of faiths and the
    least of faiths,
Enclosing worship ancient and modern
    and all between ancient and modern,
Believing I shall come again upon the
    earth after five thousand years,
Waiting responses from oracles, honoring
    the gods, saluting the sun,

Making a fetich of the first rock or
    stump, powowing with sticks in the
    circle of obis,
Helping the llama or brahmin as he trims
    the lamps of the idols,
Dancing yet through the streets in a
    phallic procession, rapt and austere in
    the woods a gymnosophist,
Drinking mead from the skull-cup, to
    Shastas and Vedas admirant, minding
    the Koran,
Walking the teokallis, spotted with gore
    from the stone and knife, beating the
    serpent-skin drum,
Accepting the Gospels, accepting him that
    was crucified, knowing assuredly that
    he is divine,
To the mass kneeling or the puritan's prayer
    rising, or sitting patiently in a pew,
Ranting and frothing in my insane crisis,
    or waiting dead-like till my spirit
    arouses me,
Looking forth on pavement and land, or
    outside of pavement and land,
Belonging to the winders of the circuit of
    circuits.

One of that centripetal and centrifugal
    gang I turn and talk like a man
    leaving charges before a journey.

173

Down-hearted doubters dull and
    excluded,
Frivolous, sullen, moping, angry, affected,
    dishearten'd, atheistical,
I know every one of you, I know the sea
    of torment, doubt, despair and
    unbelief.

How the flukes splash!
How they contort rapid as lightning, with
    spasms and spouts of blood!

Be at peace bloody flukes of doubters and
    sullen mopers,
I take my place among you as much as
    among any,
The past is the push of you, me, all,
    precisely the same,
And what is yet untried and afterward
    is for you, me, all, precisely the
    same.

I do not know what is untried and
    afterward,
But I know it will in its turn prove
    sufficient, and cannot fail.

Each who passes is consider'd, each who
    stops is consider'd, not a single one
    can it fail.

174

It cannot fail the young man who died
    and was buried,
Nor the young woman who died and was
    put by his side,
Nor the little child that peep'd in at the
    door, and then drew back and was
    never seen again,
Nor the old man who has lived without
    purpose, and feels it with bitterness
    worse than gall,
Nor him in the poor house tubercled by
    rum and the bad disorder,
Nor the numberless slaughter'd and
    wreck'd, nor the brutish koboo call'd
    the ordure of humanity,
Nor the sacs merely floating with open
    mouths for food to slip in,
Nor any thing in the earth, or down in
    the oldest graves of the earth,
Nor any thing in the myriads of spheres,
    nor the myriads of myriads that
    inhabit them,
Nor the present, nor the least wisp that is
    known.

XLIV
It is time to explain myself — let us stand
    up.

What is known I strip away,

I launch all men and women forward with
   me into the Unknown.

The clock indicates the moment — but
   what does eternity indicate?

We have thus far exhausted trillions of
   winters and summers,
There are trillions ahead, and trillions
   ahead of them.

Births have brought us richness and
   variety,
And other births will bring us richness
   and variety.

I do not call one greater and one smaller,
That which fills its period and place is
   equal to any.

Were mankind murderous or jealous upon
   you, my brother, my sister?
I am sorry for you, they are not
   murderous or jealous upon me,
All has been gentle with me, I keep no
   account with lamentation,
(What have I to do with lamentation?)

I am an acme of things accomplish'd, and
   I am encloser of things to be.

My feet strike an apex of the apices of
    the stairs,
On every step bunches of ages, and larger
    bunches between the steps,
All below duly travel'd, and still I mount
    and mount.

Rise after rise bow the phantoms behind
    me,
Afar down I see the huge first Nothing, I
    know I was even there,
I waited unseen and always, and slept
    through the lethargic mist,
And took my time, and took no hurt from
    the fetid carbon.

Long I was hugg'd close — long and
    long.

Immense have been the preparations for
    me,
Faithful and friendly the arms that have
    help'd me.

Cycles ferried my cradle, rowing and
    rowing like cheerful boatmen,
For room to me stars kept aside in their
    own rings,
They sent influences to look after what
    was to hold me.

Before I was born out of my mother
    generations guided me,
My embryo has never been torpid,
    nothing could overlay it.

For it the nebula cohered to an orb,
The long slow strata piled to rest it on,
Vast vegetables gave it sustenance,
Monstrous sauroids transported it in their
    mouths and deposited it with care.

All forces have been steadily employ'd to
    complete and delight me,
Now on this spot I stand with my robust
    soul.

XLV

O span of youth! ever-push'd elasticity!
O manhood, balanced, florid and full.

My lovers suffocate me,
Crowding my lips, thick in the pores of
    my skin,
Jostling me through streets and public
    halls, coming naked to me at night,
Crying by day *Ahoy!* from the rocks of
    the river, swinging and chirping over
    my head,
Calling my name from flower-beds, vines,
    tangled underbrush,

Lighting on every moment of my life,
Bussing my body with soft balsamic
    busses,
Noiselessly passing handfuls out of their
    hearts and giving them to be mine.

Old age superbly rising! O welcome,
    ineffable grace of dying days!

Every condition promulges not only itself,
    it promulges what grows after and
    out of itself,
And the dark hush promulges as much as
    any.

I open my scuttle at night and see the
    far-sprinkled systems,
And all I see multiplied as high as I can
    cipher edge but the rim of the farther
    systems.

Wider and wider they spread, expanding,
    always expanding,
Outward and outward and forever
    outward.

My sun has his sun and round him
    obediently wheels,
He joins with his partners a group of
    superior circuit,

And greater sets follow, making specks of
the greatest inside them.

There is no stoppage and never can be
stoppage,
If I, you, and the worlds, and all beneath
or upon their surfaces, were this
moment reduced back to a pallid
float, it would not avail in the long
run,
We should surely bring up again where
we now stand,
And surely go as much farther, and then
farther and farther.

A few quadrillions of eras, a few octillions
of cubic leagues, do not hazard the
span or make it impatient,
They are but parts, any thing is but a
part.
See ever so far, there is limitless space
outside of that,
Count ever so much, there is limitless
time around that.

My rendezvous is appointed, it is certain,
The Lord will be there and wait till I
come on perfect terms,
The great Camerado, the lover true for
whom I pine will be there.

XLVI

I know I have the best of time and space,
    and was never measured and never
    will be measured.

I tramp a perpetual journey, (come listen
    all!)
My signs are a rain-proof coat, good
    shoes, and a staff cut from the woods,
No friend of mine takes his ease in my
    chair,
I have no chair, no church, no
    philosophy,
I lead no man to a dinner-table, library,
    exchange,
But each man and each woman of you I
    lead upon a knoll,
My left hand hooking you round the
    waist,
My right hand pointing to landscapes of
    continents and the public road.
Not I, not any one else can travel that
    road for you,
You must travel it for yourself.

It is not far, it is within reach,
Perhaps you have been on it since you
    were born and did not know,
Perhaps it is everywhere on water and on
    land.

Shoulder your duds dear son, and I will
    mine, and let us hasten forth,
Wonderful cities and free nations we shall
    fetch as we go.

If you tire, give me both burdens, and the
    rest the chuff of your hand on my
    hip,
And in due time you shall repay the same
    service to me,
For after we start we never lie by again.

This day before dawn I ascended a hill
    and look'd at the crowded heaven,
And I said to my spirit *When we become
    the enfolders of those orbs, and the
    pleasure and knowledge of every
    thing in them, shall we be fill'd and
    satisfied then?*
And my spirit said *No, we but level that
    lift to pass and continue beyond.*

You are also asking me questions and I
    hear you,
I answer that I cannot answer, you must
    find out for yourself.

Sit a while dear son,
Here are biscuits to eat and here is milk
    to drink,

But as soon as you sleep and renew
  yourself in sweet clothes, I kiss you
  with a good-by kiss and open the gate
  for your egress hence.

Long enough have you dream'd
  contemptible dreams,
Now I wash the gum from your eyes,
You must habit yourself to the dazzle of
  the light and of every moment of
  your life.

Long have you timidly waded holding a
  plank by the shore,
Now I will you to be a bold swimmer,
To jump off in the midst of the
  sea, rise again, nod to me,
  shout, and laughingly dash with
  your hair.

XLVII

I am the teacher of athletes,
He that by me spreads a wider breast
  than my own proves the width of my
  own,
He most honors my style who learns
  under it to destroy the teacher.
The boy I love, the same becomes a man
  not through derived power, but in his
  own right,

Wicked rather than virtuous out of
conformity or fear,
Fond of his sweetheart, relishing well his
steak,
Unrequited love or a slight cutting him
worse than sharp steel cuts,
First-rate to ride, to fight, to hit the bull's
eye, to sail a skiff, to sing a song or
play on the banjo,
Preferring scars and the beard and faces
pitted with small-pox over all latherers,
And those well-tann'd to those that keep
out of the sun.

I teach straying from me, yet who can
stray from me?
I follow you whoever you are from the
present hour,
My words itch at your ears till you
understand them.

I do not say these things for a dollar or to
fill up the time while I wait for a boat,
(It is you talking just as much as myself, I
act as the tongue of you,
Tied in your mouth, in mine it begins to
be loosen'd.)

I swear I will never again mention love or
death inside a house,

And I swear I will never translate myself
    at all, only to him or her who
    privately stays with me in the open
    air.

If you would understand me go to the
    heights or water-shore,
The nearest gnat is an explanation, and a
    drop or motion of waves a key,
The maul, the oar, the hand-saw, second
    my words.

No shutter'd room or school can
    commune with me,
But roughs and little children better than
    they.

The young mechanic is closest to me, he
    knows me well,
The woodman that takes his axe and jug
    with him shall take me with him all
    day,
The farm-boy ploughing in the field feels
    good at the sound of my voice,
In vessels that sail my words sail, I go
    with fishermen and seamen and love
    them.

The soldier camp'd or upon the march is
    mine,

On the night ere the pending battle
    many seek me, and I do not fail
    them,
On that solemn night (it may be their
    last) those that know me seek me.

My face rubs to the hunter's face when
    he lies down alone in his blanket,
The driver thinking of me does not mind
    the jolt of his wagon,
The young mother and old mother
    comprehend me,
The girl and the wife rest the
    needle a moment and forget where
    they are,
They and all would resume what I have
    told them.

XLVIII

I have said that the soul is not more than
    the body,
And I have said that the body is not more
    than the soul,
And nothing, not God, is greater to one
    than one's self is,
And whoever walks a furlong without
    sympathy walks to his own funeral
    drest in his shroud,
And I or you pocketless of a dime may
    purchase the pick of the earth,

And to glance with an eye or show a bean
in its pod confounds the learning of
all times,
And there is no trade or employment but
the young man following it may
become a hero,
And there is no object so soft but it
makes a hub for the wheel'd universe,
And I say to any man or woman, Let
your soul stand cool and composed
before a million universes.

And I say to mankind, Be not curious
about God,
For I who am curious about each am not
curious about God,
(No array of terms can say how much I
am at peace about God and about
death.)

I hear and behold God in every object,
yet understand God not in the least,
Nor do I understand who there can be
more wonderful than myself.

Why should I wish to see God better than
this day?
I see something of God each hour
of the twenty-four, and each moment
then,

In the faces of men and women I see
    God and in my own face in the glass,
I find letters from God dropt in the
    street, and every one is sign'd by
    God's name,
And I leave them where they are, for I
    know that wheresoe'er I go,
Others will punctually come for ever and
    ever.

XLIX

And as to you Death, and you bitter hug of
    mortality, it is idle to try to alarm me.

To his work without flinching the
    accoucheur comes,
I see the elder-hand pressing receiving
    supporting,
I recline by the sills of the exquisite
    flexible doors,
And mark the outlet, and mark the relief
    and escape.

And as to you Corpse I think you are
    good manure but that does not
    offend me,
I smell the white roses sweet-scented and
    growing,
I reach to the leafy lips, I reach to the
    polish'd breasts of melons.

And as to you Life I reckon you are the
　　leavings of many deaths,
(No doubt I have died myself ten
　　thousand times before.)

I hear you whispering there O stars of
　　heaven,
O suns — O grass of graves — O
　　perpetual transfers and promotions,
If you do not say any thing how can I say
　　any thing?

Of the turbid pool that lies in the autumn
　　forest,
Of the moon that descends the steeps of
　　the soughing twilight,
Toss, sparkles of day and dusk — toss on
　　the black stems that decay in the
　　muck,
Toss to the moaning gibberish of the dry
　　limbs.

I ascend from the moon, I ascend from
　　the night,
I perceive that the ghastly glimmer is
　　noonday sunbeams reflected,

And debouch to the steady and central
　　from the offspring great or small.

L

There is that in me — I do not know
    what it is — but I know it is in me.

Wrench'd and sweaty — calm and cool
    then my body becomes,
I sleep — I sleep long.

I do not know it — it is without name —
    it is a word unsaid,
It is not in any dictionary, utterance, symbol.

Something it swings on more than the
    earth I swing on,
To it the creation is the friend whose
    embracing awakes me.

Perhaps I might tell more. Outlines! I
    plead for my brothers and sisters.

Do you see O my brothers and sisters?
It is not chaos or death — it is form,
    union, plan — it is eternal life — it is
    Happiness.

LI

The past and present wilt — I have fill'd
    them, emptied them
And proceed to fill my next fold of the
    future.

Listener up there! what have you to
 confide to me?
Look in my face while I snuff the sidle of
 evening,
(Talk honestly, no one else hears you, and
 I stay only a minute longer.)

Do I contradict myself?
Very well then I contradict myself,
(I am large, I contain multitudes.)

I concentrate toward them that are nigh, I
 wait on the door-slab.

Who has done his day's work? who
 will soonest be through with his
 supper?
Who wishes to walk with me?

Will you speak before I am gone? will you
 prove already too late?

LII
The spotted hawk swoops by and accuses
 me, he complains of my gab and my
 loitering.
I too am not a bit tamed, I too am
 untranslatable,
I sound my barbaric yawp over the roofs
 of the world.

The last scud of day holds back for me,
It flings my likeness after the rest and
    true as any on the shadow'd wilds,
It coaxes me to the vapor and the dusk.

I depart as air, I shake my white locks at
    the runaway sun,
I effuse my flesh eddies, and drift it in
    lacy jags.

I bequeath myself to the dirt to grow
    from the grass I love,
If you want me again look for me under
    your boot-soles.

You will hardly know who I am or what I
    mean,
But I shall be good health to you
    nevertheless,
And filter and fibre your blood.

Failing to fetch me at first keep
    encouraged,
Missing me one place search another,
I stop somewhere waiting for you.

1855

THE SLEEPERS

I

I wander all night in my vision,
Stepping with light feet. . . . swiftly and
    noiselessly stepping and stopping,
Bending with open eyes over the shut
    eyes of sleepers;
Wandering and confused. . . . lost to
    myself. . . . ill-assorted. . . .
    contradictory,
Pausing and gazing and bending and
    stopping.

How solemn they look there, stretched
    and still;
How quiet they breathe, the little children
    in their cradles.

The wretched features of ennuyees, the
    white features of corpses, the livid
    faces of drunkards, the sick-gray faces
    of onanists,
The gashed bodies on battlefields, the
    insane in their strong-doored rooms,
    the sacred idiots,
The newborn emerging from gates and
    the dying emerging from gates,
The night pervades them and enfolds
    them.

The married couple sleep calmly in their
    bed, he with his palm on the hip of
    the wife, and she with her palm on
    the hip of the husband,

The sisters sleep lovingly side by side in
    their bed,
The men sleep lovingly side by side in
    theirs,
And the mother sleeps with her little
    child carefully wrapped.

The blind sleep, and the deaf and dumb
    sleep,
The prisoner sleeps well in the
    prison. . . . the runaway son sleeps,
The murderer that is to be hung next
    day. . . . how does he sleep?
And the murdered person. . . . how does
    he sleep?

The female that loves unrequited sleeps,
And the male that loves unrequited sleeps;
The head of the moneymaker that plotted
    all day sleeps,
And the enraged and treacherous
    dispositions sleep.

I stand with drooping eyes by the
    worstsuffering and restless,

I pass my hands soothingly to and fro a
    few inches from them;
The restless sink in their beds. . . . they
    fitfully sleep.

The earth recedes from me into the
    night,
I saw that it was beautiful. . . . and
    I see that what is not the earth is
    beautiful.
I go from bedside to bedside. . . . I sleep
    close with the other sleepers, each in
    turn;
I dream in my dream all the dreams of
    the other dreamers,
And I become the other dreamers.

I am a dance. . . . Play up there! the fit is
    whirling me fast.

I am the everlaughing. . . . it is new
    moon and twilight,
I see the hiding of douceurs. . . . I see
    nimble ghosts whichever way I look,
Cache and cache again deep in the
    ground and sea, and where it is
    neither ground or sea.

Well do they do their jobs those
    journeymen divine,

Only from me can they hide nothing and
    would not if they could;
I reckon I am their boss, and they make
    me a pet besides,
And surround me, and lead me and run
    ahead when I walk,
And lift their cunning covers and signify
    me with stretched arms, and resume
    the way;
Onward we move, a gay gang of
    blackguards with mirthshouting music
    and wildflapping pennants of joy.

I am the actor and the actress. . . . the
    voter . . the politician,
The emigrant and the exile . . the
    criminal that stood in the box,
He who has been famous, and he who
    shall be famous after today,
The stammerer. . . . the wellformed
    person . . the wasted or feeble
    person.

I am she who adorned herself and folded
    her hair expectantly,
My truant lover has come and it is dark.

Double yourself and receive me darkness,
Receive me and my lover too. . . . he will
    not let me go without him.

I roll myself upon you as upon a bed. . . .
    I resign myself to the dusk.

He whom I call answers me and takes the
    place of my lover,
He rises with me silently from the bed.

Darkness you are gentler than my
    lover. . . . his flesh was sweaty and
    panting,
I feel the hot moisture yet that he left me.

My hands are spread forth . . I pass them
    in all directions,
I would sound up the shadowy shore to
    which you are journeying.

Be careful, darkness. . . . already, what
    was it touched me?
I thought my lover had gone. . . . else
    darkness and he are one,
I hear the heart-beat. . . . I follow . . I
    fade away.

O hotcheeked and blushing! O foolish
    hectic!
O for pity's sake, no one must see me
    now! . . . . my clothes were stolen
    while I was abed,
Now I am thrust forth, where shall I run?

197

Pier that I saw dimly last night when I
   looked from the windows,
Pier out from the main, let me catch
   myself with you and stay. . . . I will
   not chafe you;
I feel ashamed to go naked about the world,
And am curious to know where my feet
   stand. . . . and what is this flooding
   me, childhood or manhood. . . . and
   the hunger that crosses the bridge
   between.

The cloth laps a first sweet eating and
   drinking,
Laps life-swelling yolks. . . . laps ear of
   rose-corn, milky and just ripened;
The white teeth stay, and the boss-tooth
   advances in darkness,
And liquor is spilled on lips and bosoms
   by touching glasses, and the best
   liquor afterward.

II

I descend my western course. . . . my
   sinews are flaccid,
Perfume and youth course through me,
   and I am their wake.

It is my face yellow and wrinkled instead
   of the old woman's,

I sit low in a strawbottom chair and
 carefully darn my grandson's
 stockings.

It is I too. . . . the sleepless widow
 looking out on the winter midnight
I see the sparkles of starshine on the icy
 and pallid earth.

A shroud I see — and I am the
 shroud. . . . I wrap a body and lie in
 the coffin;
It is dark here underground. . . . it is not
 evil or pain here. . . . it is blank here,
 for reasons.

It seems to me that everything in the light
 and air ought to be happy;
Whoever is not in his coffin and the
 dark grave, let him know he has
 enough.

III
I see a beautiful gigantic swimmer
 swimming naked through the eddies
 of the sea,
His brown hair lies close and even to his
 head. . . . he strikes out with
 courageous arms. . . . he urges
 himself with his legs.

I see his white body. . . . I see his
  undaunted eyes;
I hate the swift-running eddies that would
  dash him headforemost on the rocks.

What are you doing you ruffianly red-
  trickled waves?
Will you kill the courageous giant? Will
  you kill him in the prime of his
  middle age?

Steady and long he struggles;
He is baffled and banged and
  bruised. . . . he holds out while his
  strength holds out,
The slapping eddies are spotted with his
  blood. . . . they bear him away. . . .
  they roll him and swing him and turn
  him:

His beautiful body is borne in the circling
  eddies. . . . it is continually bruised
  on rocks,
Swiftly and out of sight is born the brave
  corpse.

IV
I turn but do not extricate myself;
Confused. . . . a pastreading. . . .
  another, but with darkness yet.

The beach is cut by the razory
    ice-wind. . . . the wreck-guns sound,
The tempest lulls and the moon comes
    floundering through the drifts.

I look where the ship helplessly heads end
    on. . . . I hear the burst as she
    strikes. . . . I hear the howls of
    dismay. . . . they grow fainter and
    fainter.

I cannot aid with my wringing fingers;
I can but rush to the surf and let it
    drench me and freeze upon me.

I search with the crowd. . . . not one of
    the company is washed to us alive;
In the morning I help pick up the dead
    and lay them in rows in a barn.

V

Now of the old war-days . . the defeat at
    Brooklyn;
Washington stands inside the lines . . he
    stands on the entrenched hills amid a
    crowd of officers,
His face is cold and damp. . . . he cannot
    repress the weeping drops. . . . he lifts
    the glass perpetually to his eyes. . . .
    the color is blanched from his cheeks,

He sees the slaughter of the southern
  braves confided to him by their
  parents.

The same at last and at last when peace
  is declared,
 He stands in the room of the old
  tavern. . . . the wellbeloved soldiers
  all pass through.

The officers speechless and slow draw
  near in their turns,
The chief encircles their necks
  with his arm and kisses them on the
  cheek,
He kisses lightly the wet cheeks one after
  another. . . . he shakes hands and
  bids goodbye to the army.

VI

Now I tell what my mother told me today
  as we sat at dinner together,
Of when she was a nearly grown girl
  living home with her parents on the
  old homestead.

A red squaw came one breakfastime to
  the old homestead,
On her back she carried a bundle of
  rushes for rushbottoming chairs;

Her hair straight shiny coarse black and
    profuse halfenveloped her face,
Her step was free and elastic. . . . her
    voice sounded exquisitely as she
    spoke.

My mother looked in delight and
    amazement at the stranger,
She looked at the beauty of her tallborne
    face and full and pliant limbs,
The more she looked upon her she loved
    her,
Never before had she seen such
    wonderful beauty and purity;
She made her sit on a bench by the jamb
    of the fireplace . . . she cooked food
    for her,
She had no work to give her but she gave
    her remembrance and fondness.

The red squaw staid all the forenoon, and
    toward the middle of the afternoon
    she went away;
O my mother was loth to have her go away,
All the week she thought of her. . . . she
    watched for her many a month,
She remembered her many a winter and
    many a summer
But the red squaw never came nor was
    heard of there again.

Now Lucifer was not dead. . . . or if he
	was I am his sorrowful terrible heir;
I have been wronged. . . . I am
	oppressed. . . . I hate him that
	oppresses me,
I will either destroy him, or he shall
	release me.

Damn him! how he does defile me,
How he informs against my brother and
	sister and takes pay for their blood,
How he laughs when I look down the
	bend after the steamboat that carries
	away my woman.

Now the vast dusk bulk that is the
	whale's bulk. . . . it seems mine,
Warily, sportsman! though I lie so sleepy
	and sluggish, my tap is death.

VII

A show of the summer softness. . . . a
	contact of something unseen. . . . an
	amour of the light and air;
I am jealous and overwhelmed with
	friendliness,
And will go gallivant with the light and
	the air myself,
And have an unseen something to be in
	contact with them also.

O love and summer! you are in the
	dreams and in me,
Autumn and winter are in the dreams. . . .
	the farmer goes with his thrift,
The droves and crops increase. . . . the
	barns are wellfilled.

Elements merge in the night. . . . ships
	make tacks in the dreams. . . . the
	sailor sails. . . . the exile returns home,
The fugitive returns unharmed. . . . the
	immigrant is back beyond months
	and years;
The poor Irishman lives in the simple
	house of his childhood, with the
	wellknown neighbors and faces,
They warmly welcome him . . . . he is
	barefoot again. . . . he forgets he is
	welloff;

The Dutchman voyages home, and the
	Scotchman and Welchman voyage
	home . . and the native of the
	Mediterranean voyages home;
To every port of England and France and
	Spain enter wellfilled ships;
The Swiss foots it toward his hills. . . .
	the Prussian goes his way, and the
	Hungarian his way, and the Pole goes
	his way,

The Swede returns, and the Dane and
    Norwegian return.

The homeward bound and the outward
    bound,
The beautiful lost swimmer, the ennuyee,
    the onanist, the female that loves
    unrequited, the moneymaker,
The actor and actress . . those through
    with their parts and those waiting to
    commence,
The affectionate boy, the husband and
    wife, the voter, the nominee that is
    chosen and the nominee that has
    failed,
The great already known, and the great
    anytime after to day,
The stammerer, the sick, the perfectformed,
    the homely,
The criminal that stood in the box, the
    judge that sat and sentenced him, the
    fluent lawyers, the jury, the audience,
The laugher and weeper, the dancer, the
    midnight-widow, the red squaw,
The consumptive, the erysipalite, the
    idiot, he that is wronged,
The antipodes, and every one between
    this and them in the dark,
I swear they are averaged now. . . . one is
    no better than the other,

The night and sleep have likened them
    and restored them.

I swear they are all beautiful,
Every one that sleeps is beautiful. . . .
    every thing in the dim night is
    beautiful,
The wildest and bloodiest is over and all
    is peace.

Peace is always beautiful,
The myth of heaven indicates peace and
    night.

The myth of heaven indicates
    the soul;
The soul is always beautiful. . . . it
    appears more or it appears less. . . . it
    comes or lags behind,
It comes from its embowered garden and
    looks pleasantly on itself and encloses
    the world;
Perfect and clean the genitals previously
    jetting, and perfect and clean the
    womb cohering,
The head wellgrown and proportioned
    and plumb, and the bowels and joints
    proportioned and plumb.

The soul is always beautiful,

The universe is duly in order. . . . every
    thing is in its place,
What is arrived is in its place, and what
    waits is in its place;
The twisted skull waits. . . . the watery or
    rotten blood waits,
The child of the glutton or venerealee
    waits long, and the child of the
    drunkard waits long, and the
    drunkard himself waits long,
The sleepers that lived and died wait. . . .
    the far advanced are to go on in their
    turns, and the far behind are to go on
    in their turns,
The diverse shall be no less diverse, but
    they shall flow and unite. . . . they
    unite now.

VIII

The sleepers are very beautiful as they lie
    unclothed,
They flow hand in hand over the whole
    earth from east to west as they lie
    unclothed;
The Asiatic and African are hand in hand
    . . the European and American are
    hand in hand,
Learned and unlearned are hand in hand
    . . and male and female are hand in
    hand;

The bare arm of the girl crosses the bare
breast of her lover. . . . they press
close without lust. . . . his lips press
her neck,

The father holds his grown or ungrown
son in his arms with measureless
love. . . . and the son holds the father
in his arms with measureless love,

The white hair of the mother shines on
the white wrist of the daughter,

The breath of the boy goes with the
breath of the man. . . . friend is
inarmed by friend,

The scholar kisses the teacher and the
teacher kisses the scholar. . . . the
wronged is made right,

The call of the slave is one with the
master's call . . and the master salutes
the slave,

The felon steps forth from the
prison. . . . the insane becomes
sane. . . . the suffering of sick persons
is relieved,

The sweatings and fevers stop . . the throat
that was unsound is sound . . the
lungs of the consumptive are resumed
. . the poor distressed head is free,

The joints of the rheumatic move as
smoothly as ever, and smoother than
ever,

Stiflings and passages open. . . . the
    paralysed become supple,
The swelled and convulsed and congested
    awake to themselves in condition,
They pass the invigoration of the night
    and the chemistry of the night and
    awake.

I too pass from the night;
I stay awhile away O night, but I return
    to you again and love you;
Why should I be afraid to trust myself to
    you?

I am not afraid. . . . I have been well
    brought forward by you;
I love the rich running day, but I do not
    desert her in whom I lay so long:
I know not how I came of you, and I know
    not where I go with you. . . . but I
    know I came well and shall go well.

I will stop only a time with the night. . . .
    and rise betimes.

I will duly pass the day O my mother and
    duly return to you;
Not you will yield forth the dawn again
    more surely than you will yield forth
    me again,

Not the womb yield the babe in its time
more surely than I shall be yielded
from you in my time.

1855

PASSAGE TO INDIA

I

Singing my days,
Singing the great achievements of the
    present,
Singing the strong light works of
    engineers,
Our modern wonders, (the antique
    ponderous Seven outvied,)
In the Old World the east the Suez canal,
The New by its mighty railroad spann'd,
The seas inlaid with eloquent gentle
    wires;
Yet first to sound, and ever sound, the
    cry with thee O soul,
The Past! the Past! the Past!

The Past — the dark unfathom'd
    retrospect!
The teeming gulf — the sleepers and the
    shadows!
The past — the infinite greatness of the
    past!
For what is the present after all but a
    growth out of the past?
(As a projectile form'd, impell'd, passing a
    certain line, still keeps on,
So the present, utterly form'd, impell'd by
    the past.)

II

Passage O soul to India!
Eclaircise the myths Asiatic, the primitive
    fables.
Not you alone proud truths of the world,
Nor you alone ye facts of modern
    science,
But myths and fables of eld, Asia's,
    Africa's fables,
The far-darting beams of the spirit, the
    unloos'd dreams,
The deep diving bibles and legends,
The daring plots of the poets, the elder
    religions;
O you temples fairer than lilies pour'd
    over by the rising sun!
O you fables spurning the known, eluding
    the hold of the known, mounting to
    heaven!
You lofty and dazzling towers, pinnacled,
    red as roses, burnish'd with gold!
Towers of fables immortal fashion'd from
    mortal dreams!
You too I welcome and fully the same as
    the rest!
You too with joy I sing.

Passage to India!
Lo, soul, seest thou not God's purpose
    from the first?

The earth to be spann'd, connected by
    network,
The races, neighbors, to marry and be
    given in marriage,

The oceans to be cross'd, the distant
    brought near,
The lands to be welded together.

A worship new I sing,
You captains, voyagers, explorers, yours,
You engineers, you architects, machinists,
    yours,
You, not for trade or transportation only,
But in God's name, and for thy sake
    O soul.

III

Passage to India!
Lo soul for thee of tableaus twain,
I see in one the Suez canal initiated,
    open'd,
I see the procession of steamships, the
    Empress Eugenie's leading the van,
I mark from on deck the strange
    landscape, the pure sky, the level
    sand in the distance,
I pass swifly the picturesque groups, the
    workmen gather'd,
The gigantic dredging machines.

In one again, different, (yet thine, all
thine, O soul, the same,)
I see over my own continent the Pacific
railroad surmounting every barrier,
I see continual trains of cars winding
along the Platte carrying freight and
passengers,
I hear the locomotives rushing and
roaring, and the shrill steam-whistle,
I hear the echoes reverberate through the
grandest scenery in the world,
I cross the Laramie plains, I note
the rocks in grotesque shapes, the
buttes,
I see the plentiful larkspur and wild
onions, the barren, colorless, sage-
deserts,
I see in glimpses afar or towering
immediately above me the great
mountains, I see the Wind river and
the Wahsatch mountains,
I see the Monument mountain and the
Eagle's Nest, I pass the Promontory, I
ascend the Nevadas,
I scan the noble Elk mountain and wind
around its base,
I see the Humboldt range, I thread the
valley and cross the river,
I see the clear waters of lake Tahoe, I see
forests of majestic pines,

Or crossing the great desert, the alkaline
    plains, I behold enchanting mirages
    of waters and meadows,
Marking through these and after all, in
    duplicate slender lines,
Bridging the three or four thousand miles
    of land travel,
Tying the Eastern to the Western sea,
The road between Europe and Asia.

(Ah Genoese thy dream! thy dream!
Centuries after thou art laid in thy grave,
The shore thou foundest verifies thy
    dream.)

IV

Passage to India!
Struggles of many a captain, tales of
    many a sailor dead,
Over my mood stealing and spreading
    they come,
Like clouds and cloudlets in the
    unreach'd sky.
Along all history, down the slopes,
As a rivulet running, sinking now, and
    now again to the surface rising,
A ceaseless thought, a varied train — lo,
    soul, to thee, thy sight, they rise,
The plans, the voyages again, the
    expeditions;

Again Vasco de Gama sails forth,
Again the knowledge gain'd, the mariner's
  compass,
Lands found and nations born, thou born
  America,
For purpose vast, man's long probation
  fill'd,
Thou rondure of the world at last
  accomplish'd.

V

O vast Rondure, swimming in space,
Cover'd all over with visible power and
  beauty,
Alternate light and day and the teeming
  spiritual darkness,
Unspeakable high processions of
  sun and moon and countless stars
  above,
Below, the manifold grass and waters,
  animals, mountains, trees,
With inscrutable purpose, some hidden
  prophetic intention,
Now first it seems my thought begins to
  span thee.

Down from the gardens of Asia
  descending radiating,
Adam and Eve appear, then their myriad
  progeny after them,

Wandering, yearning, curious, with
    restless explorations,
With questionings, baffled, formless,
    feverish, with never-happy hearts,
With that sad incessant refrain,
    Wherefore unsatisfied soul? and
    Whither O mocking life?

Ah who shall soothe these feverish
    children?
Who justify these restless explorations?
Who speak the secret of impassive earth?
Who bind it to us? what is this separate
    Nature so unnatural?
What is this earth to our affections?
    (unloving earth, without a throb to
    answer ours,
Cold earth, the place of graves.)

Yet soul be sure the first intent remains,
    and shall be carried out,
Perhaps even now the time has arrived.

After the seas are all cross'd, (as they
    seem already cross'd,)
After the great captains and engineers
    have accomplish'd their work,
After the noble inventors, after the
    scientists, the chemist, the geologist,
    ethnologist,

Finally shall come the poet worthy that
    name,
The true son of God shall come singing
    his songs.

Then not your deeds only O voyagers, O
    scientist and inventors, shall be
    justified,
All these hearts as of fretted children
    shall be sooth'd,
All affection shall be fully responded to,
    the secret shall be told,
All these separations and gaps shall be
    taken up and hook'd and link'd
    together,

The whole earth, this cold, impassive,
    voiceless earth, shall be completely
    justified,
Trinitas divine shall be gloriously
    accomplish'd and compacted by the
    true son of God, the poet,
(He shall indeed pass the straits and
    conquer the mountains,
He shall double the cape of Good Hope
    to some purpose,)
Nature and Man shall be disjoin'd and
    diffused no more,
The true son of God shall absolutely fuse
    them.

VI

Year at whose wide-flung door I sing!
Year of the purpose accomplish'd!
Year of the marriage of continents,
    climates and oceans!
(No mere doge of Venice now wedding
    the Adriatic,)
I see O year in you the vast terraqueous
    globe given and giving all,
Europe to Asia, Africa join'd, and they to
    the New World,
The lands, geographies, dancing before
    you, holding a festival garland,
As brides and bridegrooms hand in hand.

Passage to India!
Cooling airs from Caucasus far, soothing
    cradle of man,
The river Euphrates flowing, the past lit
    up again.

Lo soul, the retrospect brought forward,
The old, most populous, wealthiest of
    earth's lands,
The streams of the Indus and the Ganges
    and their many affluents,
(I my shores of America walking to-day
    behold, resuming all,)
The tale of Alexander on his warlike
    marches suddenly dying,

On one side China and on the other side
 Persia and Arabia,
To the south the great seas and the bay of
 Bengal,
The flowing literatures, tremendous epics,
 religions, castes,
Old occult Brahma interminably far back,
 the tender and junior Buddha,
Central and southern empires and all
 their belongings, possessors,
The wars of Tamerlane, the reign of
 Aurungzebe,
The traders, rulers, explorers, Moslems,
 Venetians, Byzantium, the Arabs,
 Portuguese,
The first travelers famous yet, Marco
 Polo, Batouta the Moor,
Doubts to be solv'd, the map incognita,
 blanks to be fill'd,
The foot of man unstay'd, the hands
 never at rest,
Thyself O soul that will not brook a
 challenge.

The mediæval navigators rise before me,
The world of 1492, with its awaken'd
 enterprise,
Something swelling in humanity now like
 the sap of the earth in spring,
The sunset splendor of chivalry declining.

And who art thou sad shade?
Gigantic, visionary, thyself a visionary,
With majestic limbs and pious beaming
    eyes,
Spreading around with every look of
    thine a golden world,
Enhuing it with gorgeous hues.

As the chief histrion,
Down to the footlights walks in some
    great scena,
Dominating the rest I see the Admiral
    himself,
(History's type of courage, action, faith,)
Behold him sail from Palos leading his
    little fleet,
His voyage behold, his return, his great
    fame,
His misfortunes, calumniators, behold
    him a prisoner, chain'd,
Behold his dejection, poverty, death.
(Curious in time I stand, noting the
    efforts of heroes,
Is the deferment long? bitter the slander,
    poverty, death?
Lies the seed unreck'd for centuries
    in the ground? lo, to God's due
    occasion,
Uprising in the night, it sprouts, blooms,
And fills the earth with use and beauty.)

VII

Passage indeed O soul to primal thought,
Not lands and seas alone, thy own clear
  freshness,
The young maturity of brood and bloom,
To realms of budding bibles.

O soul, repressless, I with thee and thou
  with me,
Thy circumnavigation of the world begin,
Of man, the voyage of his mind's return,
To reason's early paradise,
Back, back to wisdom's birth, to innocent
  intuitions,
Again with fair creation.

VIII

O we can wait no longer,
We too take ship O soul,
Joyous we too launch out on trackless
  seas,
Fearless for unknown shores on waves of
  ecstasy to sail,
Amid the wafting winds, (thou pressing
  me to thee, I thee to me, O soul,)
Caroling free, singing our song of God,
Chanting our chant of pleasant
  exploration.

With laugh and many a kiss,

(Let others deprecate, let others weep for
    sin, remorse, humiliation,)
O soul thou pleasest me, I thee.

Ah more than any priest O soul we too
    believe in God,
But with the mystery of God we dare not
    dally.

O soul thou pleasest me, I thee,
Sailing these seas or on the hills, or
    waking in the night,
Thoughts, silent thoughts, of Time and
    Space and Death, like waters flowing,
Bear me indeed as through the regions
    infinite,
Whose air I breathe, whose ripples hear,
    lave me all over,
Bathe me O God in thee, mounting to
    thee,
I and my soul to range in range of thee.

O Thou transcendent,
Nameless, the fibre and the breath,
Light of the light, shedding forth
    universes, thou centre of them,
Thou mightier centre of the true, the
    good, the loving,
Thou moral, spiritual fountain —
    affection's source — thou reservoir,

(O pensive soul of me — O thirst
    unsatisfied — waitest not there?
Waitest not haply for us somewhere there
    the Comrade perfect?)
Thou pulse — thou motive of the stars,
    suns, systems,
That, circling, move in order, safe
    harmonious,
Athwart the shapeless vastnesses of space,
How should I think, how breathe a single
    breath, how speak, if, out of myself,
I could not launch, to those, superior
    universes?

Swiftly I shrivel at the thought of God,
At Nature and its wonders, Time and
    Space and Death,
But that I, turning, call to thee O soul,
    thou actual Me,
And lo, thou gently masterest the orbs,
Thou matest Time, smilest content at
    Death,
And fillest, swellest full the vastnesses of
    Space.

Greater than stars or suns,
Bounding O soul thou journeyest forth;
What love than thine and ours could
    wider amplify?

What aspirations, wishes, outvie thine and
    ours O soul?
What dreams of the ideal? what plans of
    purity, perfection, strength?
What cheerful willingness for others' sake
    to give up all?
For others' sake to suffer all?

Reckoning ahead O soul, when thou, the
    time achiev'd,
The seas all cross'd, weather'd the capes,
    the voyage done,
Surrounded, copest, frontest God,
    yieldest, the aim attain'd,
As fill'd with friendship, love complete,
    the Elder Brother found,
The Younger melts in fondness in his
    arms.

IX

Passage to more than India!
Are thy wings plumed indeed for such far
    flights?
O soul, voyagest thou indeed on voyages
    like those?
Disportest thou on waters such as
    those?
Soundest below the Sanscrit and the
    Vedas?
Then have they bent unleash'd.

Passage to you, your shores, ye aged
    fierce enigmas!
Passage to you, to mastership of you, ye
    strangling problems!
You, strew'd with the wrecks of skeletons,
    that, living, never reach'd you.

Passage to more than India!
O secret of the earth and sky!
Of you O waters of the sea! O winding
    creeks and rivers!
Of you O woods and fields! of you strong
    mountains of my land!
Of you O prairies! of you gray rocks!
O morning red! O clouds! O rain and
    snows!
O day and night, passage to you!

O sun and moon and all you stars! Sirius
    and Jupiter!
Passage to you!

Passage, immediate passage! the blood
    burns in my veins!
Away O soul! hoist instantly the
    anchor!
Cut the hawsers — haul out — shake out
    every sail!
Have we not stood here like trees in the
    ground long enough?

Have we not grovel'd here long enough,
   eating and drinking like mere brutes?
Have we not darken'd and dazed
   ourselves with books long enough?

Sail forth — steer for the deep waters
   only,
Reckless O soul, exploring, I with thee,
   and thou with me,
For we are bound where mariner has not
   yet dared to go,
And we will risk the ship, ourselves and
   all.

O my brave soul!
O farther farther sail!
O daring joy, but safe! are they not all the
   seas of God?
O farther, farther, farther sail!

1871

OUT OF THE CRADLE ENDLESSLY ROCKING

Out of the cradle endlessly rocking,
Out of the mocking-bird's throat, the
    musical shuttle,
Out of the Ninth-month midnight,
Over the sterile sands and the fields
    beyond, where the child leaving his
    bed wander'd alone, bareheaded,
    barefoot,
Down from the shower'd halo,
Up from the mystic play of shadows
    twining and twisting as if they were
    alive,
Out from the patches of briers and
    blackberries,
From the memories of the bird that
    chanted to me,
From your memories sad brother, from
    the fitful risings and fallings I heard,
From under that yellow half-moon late-
    risen and swollen as if with tears,
From those beginning notes of yearning
    and love there in the mist,
From the thousand responses of my heart
    never to cease,
From the myriad thence-arous'd words,
From the word stronger and more
    delicious than any,

From such as now they start the scene
    revisiting,
As a flock, twittering, rising, or overhead
    passing,
Borne hither, ere all eludes me, hurriedly,
A man, yet by these tears a little boy
    again,
Throwing myself on the sand, confronting
    the waves,
I, chanter of pains and joys, uniter of here
    and hereafter,
Taking all hints to use them, but swiftly
    leaping beyond them,
A reminiscence sing.

Once Paumanok,
When the lilac-scent was in the air and
    Fifth-month grass was growing,
Up this seashore in some briers,
Two feather'd guests from Alabama, two
    together,
And their nest, and four light-green eggs
    spotted with brown,
And every day the he-bird to and fro near
    at hand,
And every day the she-bird crouch'd on
    her nest, silent, with bright eyes,
And every day I, a curious boy, never too
    close, never disturbing them,
Cautiously peering, absorbing, translating.

Shine! shine! shine!
Pour down your warmth, great sun!
While we bask, we two together.

Two together!
Winds blow south, or winds blow north,
Day come white, or night come black,
Home, or rivers and mountains from
        home,
Singing all time, minding no time,
While we two keep together.

Till of a sudden,
May-be kill'd, unknown to her mate,
One forenoon the she-bird crouch'd not
        on the nest,
Nor return'd that afternoon, nor the next,
Nor ever appear'd again.

And thenceforward all summer in the
        sound of the sea,
And at night under the full of the moon
        in calmer weather,
Over the hoarse surging of the sea,
Or flitting from brier to brier by day,
I saw, I heard at intervals the remaining
        one, the he-bird,
The solitary guest from Alabama.

Blow! blow! blow!

Blow up sea-winds along Paumanok's
*   shore;*
I wait and I wait till you blow my mate to
*   me.*

Yes, when the stars glisten'd,
All night long on the prong of a
    moss-scallop'd stake,
Down almost amid the slapping waves,
Sat the lone singer wonderful causing
    tears.

He call'd on his mate,
He pour'd forth the meanings which I of
    all men know.

Yes my brother I know,
The rest might not, but I have treasur'd
    every note,
For more than once dimly down to the
    beach gliding,
Silent, avoiding the moonbeams, blending
    myself with the shadows,
Recalling now the obscure shapes, the
    echoes, the sounds and sights after
    their sorts,
The white arms out in the breakers
    tirelessly tossing, I, with bare feet, a
    child, the wind wafting my hair,
Listen'd long and long.

Listen'd to keep, to sing, now translating
    the notes,
Following you my brother.

Soothe! soothe! soothe!
Close on its wave soothes the wave
    behind,
And again another behind embracing and
    lapping, every one close,
But my love soothes not me, not me.

Low hangs the moon, it rose late,
It is lagging — O I think it is heavy with
    love, with love.

O madly the sea pushes upon the land,
With love, with love.

O night! do I not see my love fluttering
    out among the breakers?
What is that little black thing I see there
    in the white?

Loud! loud! loud!
Loud I call to you, my love!

High and clear I shoot my voice over the
    waves,
Surely you must know who is here, is here,
You must know who I am, my love.

Low-hanging moon!
What is that dusky spot in your brown
*   yellow?*
O it is the shape, the shape of
*   my mate!*
O moon do not keep her from me any
*   longer.*

Land! land! O land!
Whichever way I turn, O I think you
*   could give me my mate back again if*
*   you only would,*
For I am almost sure I see her dimly
*   whichever way I look.*

O rising stars!
Perhaps the one I want so much will
*   rise, will rise with some of you.*

O throat! O trembling throat!
Sound clearer through the atmosphere!
Pierce the woods, the earth,
Somewhere listening to catch you must
*   be the one I want.*

Shake out carols!
Solitary here, the night's carols!
Carols of lonesome love! death's carols!
Carols under that lagging, yellow, waning
*   moon!*

O under that moon where she droops
    almost down into the sea!
O reckless despairing carols.

But soft! sink low!
Soft! let me just murmur,
And do you wait a moment you
    husky-nois'd sea,
For somewhere I believe I heard my
    mate responding to me,
So faint, I must be still, be still to listen,
But not altogether still, for then she might
    not come immediately to me.

Hither my love!
Here I am! here!
With this just-sustain'd note I announce
    myself to you,
This gentle call is for you my love, for
    you.

Do not be decoy'd elsewhere,
That is the whistle of the wind, it is not
    my voice,
That is the fluttering, the fluttering of the
    spray,
Those are the shadows of leaves.

O darkness! O in vain!
O I am very sick and sorrowful.

O brown halo in the sky near the moon,
    drooping upon the sea!
O troubled reflection in the sea!
O throat! O throbbing heart!
And I singing uselessly, uselessly all the
    night.

O past! O happy life! O songs of joy!
In the air, in the woods, over fields,
Loved! loved! loved! loved! loved!
But my mate no more, no more with me!
We two together no more.

The aria sinking,
All else continuing, the stars shining,
The winds blowing, the notes of the bird
    continuous echoing,
With angry moans the fierce old mother
    incessantly moaning,
On the sands of Paumanok's shore gray
    and rustling,
The yellow half-moon enlarged, sagging
    down, drooping, the face of the sea
    almost touching,
The boy ecstatic, with his bare feet the
    waves, with his hair the atmosphere
    dallying,
The love in the heart long pent, now
    loose, now at last tumultuously
    bursting,

The aria's meaning, the ears, the soul,
    swiftly depositing,
The strange tears down the cheeks
    coursing,
The colloquy there, the trio, each uttering,
The undertone, the savage old mother
    incessantly crying,
To the boy's soul's questions sullenly
    timing, some drown'd secret hissing,
To the outsetting bard.

Demon or bird! (said the boy's soul,)
Is it indeed toward your mate you sing?
    or is it really to me?
For I, that was a child, my tongue's use
    sleeping, now I have heard you,
Now in a moment I know what I am for,
    I awake,
And already a thousand singers, a
    thousand songs, clearer, louder and
    more sorrowful than yours,
A thousand warbling echoes have started
    to life within me, never to die.

O you singer solitary, singing by yourself,
    projecting me,
O solitary me listening, never more shall I
    cease perpetuating you,
Never more shall I escape, never more
    the reverberations,

Never more the cries of unsatisfied love
    be absent from me,
Never again leave me to be the peaceful
    child I was before what there in the
    night,
By the sea under the yellow and sagging
    moon,
The messenger there arous'd, the fire, the
    sweet hell within,
The unknown want, the destiny of me.

O give me the clew! (it lurks in the night
    here somewhere,)
O if I am to have so much, let me have
    more!

A word then, (for I will conquer it,)
The word final, superior to all,
Subtle, sent up — what is it? — I listen;
Are you whispering it, and have been all
    the time, you sea-waves?
Is that it from your liquid rims and wet
    sands?

Whereto answering, the sea,
Delaying not, hurrying not,
Whisper'd me through the night, and very
    plainly before daybreak,
Lisp'd to me the low and delicious word
    death,

And again death, death, death, death,
Hissing melodious, neither like the bird
    nor like my arous'd child's heart,
But edging near as privately for me
    rustling at my feet,
Creeping thence steadily up to my ears
    and laying me softly all over,
Death, death, death, death, death.

Which I do not forget,
But fuse the song of my dusky demon
    and brother,
That he sang to me in the moonlight on
    Paumanok's gray beach,
With the thousand responsive songs at
    random,
My own songs awaked from that hour,
And with them the key, the word up from
    the waves,
The word of the sweetest song and all
    songs,
That strong and delicious word which,
    creeping to my feet,
(Or like some old crone rocking the
    cradle, swathed in sweet garments,
    bending aside,)
The sea whisper'd me.

1859

WHEN LILACS LAST IN THE DOORYARD BLOOM'D

I

When lilacs last in the dooryard bloom'd,
And the great star early droop'd in the
    western sky in the night,
I mourn'd, and yet shall mourn with
    ever-returning spring.

Ever-returning spring, trinity sure to me
    you bring,
Lilac blooming perennial and drooping
    star in the west,
And thought of him I love.

II

O powerful western fallen star!
O shades of night — O moody, tearful
    night!
O great star disappear'd — O the black
    murk that hides the star!
O cruel hands that hold me powerless —
    O helpless soul of me!
O harsh surrounding cloud that will not
    free my soul.

III

In the dooryard fronting an old farm-house
    near the white-wash'd palings,

Stands the lilac-bush tall-growing with
  heart-shaped leaves of rich green,
With many a pointed blossom rising
  delicate, with the perfume strong I
  love,
With every leaf a miracle — and from
  this bush in the dooryard,
With delicate-color'd blossoms and heart-
  shaped leaves of rich green,
A sprig with its flower I break.

IV
In the swamp in secluded recesses,
A shy and hidden bird is warbling
  a song.

Solitary the thrush,
The hermit withdrawn to himself,
  avoiding the settlements,
Sings by himself a song.

Song of the bleeding throat,
Death's outlet song of life, (for well dear
  brother I know,
If thou wast not granted to sing thou
  would'st surely die.)

V
Over the breast of the spring, the land,
  amid cities,

Amid lanes and through old woods,
    where lately the violets peep'd from
    the ground, spotting the gray debris,
Amid the grass in the fields each side of
    the lanes, passing the endless grass,
Passing the yellow-spear'd wheat,
    every grain from its shroud in the
    dark-brown fields uprisen,
Passing the apple-tree blows of white and
    pink in the orchards,
Carrying a corpse to where it shall rest in
    the grave,
Night and day journeys a coffin.

VI

Coffin that passes through lanes and
    streets,
Through day and night with the great
    cloud darkening the land,
With the pomp of the inloop'd flags with
    the cities draped in black,
With the show of the States themselves as
    of crape-veil'd women standing,
With processions long and winding and
    the flambeaus of the night,
With the countless torches lit, with the
    silent sea of faces and the unbared
    heads,
With the waiting depot, the arriving
    coffin, and the sombre faces,

With dirges through the night, with the
    thousand voices rising strong and
    solemn,
With all the mournful voices of the dirges
    pour'd around the coffin,
The dim-lit churches and the shuddering
    organs — where amid these you
    journey,
With the tolling tolling bells' perpetual
    clang,
Here, coffin that slowly passes,
I give you my sprig of lilac.

VII

(Nor for you, for one alone,
Blossoms and branches green to coffins
    all I bring,
For fresh as the morning, thus would I
    chant a song for you O sane and
    sacred death.

All over bouquets of roses,
O death, I cover you over with roses and
    early lilies,
But mostly and now the lilac that blooms
    the first,
Copious I break, I break the sprigs from
    the bushes,
With loaded arms I come, pouring for you,
For you and the coffins all of you O death.)

VIII

O western orb sailing the heaven,
Now I know what you must have meant
    as a month since I walk'd,
As I walk'd in silence the transparent
    shadowy night,
As I saw you had something to tell as you
    bent to me night after night,
As you droop'd from the sky low down as
    if to my side, (while the other stars
    all look'd on,)
As we wander'd together the solemn
    night, (for something I know not
    what kept me from sleep,)
As the night advanced, and I saw on the
    rim of the west how full you were of
    woe,
As I stood on the rising ground in the
    breeze in the cool transparent night,
As I watch'd where you pass'd and was
    lost in the netherward black of the
    night,
As my soul in its trouble dissatisfied sank,
    as where you sad orb,
Concluded, dropt in the night, and was gone.

IX

Sing on there in the swamp,
O singer bashful and tender, I hear your
    notes, I hear your call,

I hear, I come presently, I understand
   you,
But a moment I linger, for the lustrous
   star has detain'd me,
The star my departing comrade holds and
   detains me.

X

O how shall I warble myself for the dead
   one there I loved?
And how shall I deck my song for the
   large sweet soul that has gone?
And what shall my perfume be for the
   grave of him I love?

Sea-winds blown from east and west,
Blown from the Eastern sea and blown
   from the Western sea, till there on the
   prairies meeting,
These and with these and the breath of
   my chant,
I'll perfume the grave of him I love.

XI

O what shall I hang on the chamber
   walls?
And what shall the pictures be that I
   hang on the walls,
To adorn the burial-house of him
   I love?

245

Pictures of growing spring and farms and
　　homes,
With the Fourth-month eve at sundown,
　　and the gray smoke lucid and bright,
With floods of the yellow gold of the
　　gorgeous, indolent, sinking sun,
　　burning, expanding the air,
With the fresh sweet herbage under foot,
　　and the pale green leaves of the trees
　　prolific,
In the distance the flowing glaze, the
　　breast of the river, with a wind-
　　dapple here and there,
With ranging hills on the banks, with
　　many a line against the sky, and
　　shadows,
And the city at hand with dwellings so
　　dense, and stacks of chimneys,
And all the scenes of life and the
　　workshops, and the workmen
　　homeward returning.

XII

Lo, body and soul — this land,
My own Manhattan with spires, and the
　　sparkling and hurrying tides, and the
　　ships,
The varied and ample land, the South
　　and the North in the light, Ohio's
　　shores and flashing Missouri,

And ever the far-spreading prairies
    cover'd with grass and corn.

Lo, the most excellent sun so calm and
    haughty,
The violet and purple morn with just-felt
    breezes,
The gentle soft-born measureless light,
The miracle spreading bathing all, the
    fulfill'd noon,
The coming eve delicious, the welcome
    night and the stars,
Over my cities shining all, enveloping
    man and land.

XIII

Sing on, sing on you gray-brown bird,
Sing from the swamps, the recesses, pour
    your chant from the bushes,
Limitless out of the dusk, out of the
    cedars and pines.

Sing on dearest brother, warble your
    reedy song,
Loud human song, with voice of
    uttermost woe.

O liquid and free and tender!
O wild and loose to my soul — O
    wondrous singer!

You only I hear — yet the star holds me,
	(but will soon depart,)
Yet the lilac with mastering odor holds me.

XIV

Now while I sat in the day and look'd
	forth,
In the close of the day with its light and
	the fields of spring, and the farmers
	preparing their crops,
In the large unconscious scenery of my
	land with its lakes and forests,
In the heavenly aerial beauty, (after the
	perturb'd winds and the storms,)
Under the arching heavens of the
	afternoon swift passing, and the
	voices of children and women,
The many-moving sea-tides, and I saw
	the ships how they sail'd,
And the summer approaching with
	richness, and the fields all busy with
	labor,
And the infinite separate houses, how
	they all went on, each with its meals
	and minutia of daily usages,
And the streets how their throbbings
	throbb'd, and the cities pent — lo,
	then and there,
Falling upon them all and among them
	all, enveloping me with the rest,

Appear'd the cloud, appear'd the long
	black trail,
And I knew death, its thought, and the
	sacred knowledge of death.

Then with the knowledge of death as
	walking one side of me,
And the thought of death close-walking
	the other side of me,
And I in the middle as with companions,
	and as holding the hands of
	companions,
I fled forth to the hiding receiving night
	that talks not,
Down to the shores of the water, the path
	by the swamp in the dimness,
To the solemn shadowy cedars and
	ghostly pines so still.

And the singer so shy to the rest receiv'd
	me,
The gray-brown bird I know receiv'd us
	comrades three,
And he sang the carol of death, and a
	verse for him I love.

From deep secluded recesses,
From the fragrant cedars and the ghostly
	pines so still,
Came the carol of the bird.

And the charm of the carol rapt me,
As I held as if by their hands my
   comrades in the night,
And the voice of my spirit tallied the song
   of the bird.

Come lovely and soothing death,
Undulate round the world, serenely
   arriving, arriving,
In the day, in the night, to all, to each,
Sooner or later delicate death.

Prais'd be the fathomless universe,
For life and joy, and for objects and
   knowledge curious,
And for love, sweet love — but praise!
   praise! praise!
For the sure-enwinding arms of cool-
   enfolding death.

Dark mother always gliding near with soft
   feet,
Have none chanted for thee a chant of
   fullest welcome?
Then I chant it for thee, I glorify thee
   above all,
I bring thee a song that when thou must
   indeed come, come unfalteringly.

Approach strong deliveress,

When it is so, when thou hast taken
       them I joyously sing the dead,
Lost in the loving floating ocean of thee,
Laved in the flood of thy bliss
       O death.

From me to thee glad serenades,
Dances for thee I propose saluting thee,
       adornments and feastings for thee,
And the sights of the open landscape
       and the high-spread sky are fitting,
And life and the fields, and the huge and
       thoughtful night.

The night in silence under many a star,
The ocean shore and the husky
       whispering wave whose voice I know,
And the soul turning to thee O vast and
       well-veil'd death,
And the body gratefully nestling close to
       thee.

Over the tree-tops I float thee a song,
Over the rising and sinking waves, over
       the myriad fields and the prairies
       wide,
Over the dense-pack'd cities all and the
       teeming wharves and ways,
I float this carol with joy, with joy to thee
       O death.

To the tally of my soul,
Loud and strong kept up the gray-brown
    bird,
With pure deliberate notes spreading
    filling the night.

Loud in the pines and cedars dim,
Clear in the freshness moist and the
    swamp-perfume,
And I with my comrades there in the
    night.

While my sight that was bound in my
    eyes unclosed,
As to long panoramas of visions.

And I saw askant the armies,
I saw as in noiseless dreams hundreds of
    battle-flags,
Borne through the smoke of the battles
    and pierc'd with missiles I saw them,
And carried hither and yon through the
    smoke, and torn and bloody,
And at last but a few shreds left on the
    staffs, (and all in silence,)
And the staffs all splinter'd and broken.
I saw battle-corpses, myriads of them,
And the white skeletons of young men, I
    saw them,

I saw the debris and debris of all the slain
    soldiers of the war,
But I saw they were not as was thought,
They themselves were fully at rest, they
    suffer'd not,
The living remain'd and suffer'd, the
    mother suffer'd,
And the wife and the child and the
    musing comrade suffer'd,
And the armies that remain'd suffer'd.

XVI

Passing the visions, passing the night,
Passing, unloosing the hold of my
    comrades' hands,
Passing the song of the hermit bird and
    the tallying song of my soul,
Victorious song, death's outlet song, yet
    varying ever-altering song,
As low and wailing, yet clear the notes,
    rising and falling, flooding the night,
Sadly sinking and fainting, as warning
    and warning, and yet again bursting
    with joy,
Covering the earth and filling the spread
    of the heaven,
As that powerful psalm in the night I
    heard from recesses,
Passing, I leave thee lilac with
    heart-shaped leaves,

I leave thee there in the door-yard,
    blooming, returning with spring.

I cease from my song for thee,
From my gaze on thee in the west, fronting
    the west, communing with thee,
O comrade lustrous with silver face in the
    night.

Yet each to keep and all, retrievements
    out of the night,
The song, the wondrous chant of the
    gray-brown bird,
And the tallying chant, the echo arous'd
    in my soul,
With the lustrous and drooping star with
    the countenance full of woe,
With the holders holding my hand
    nearing the call of the bird,
Comrades mine and I in the midst, and
    their memory ever to keep, for the
    dead I loved so well,
For the sweetest, wisest soul of all my
    days and lands — and this for his
    dear sake,
Lilac and star and bird twined with the
    chant of my soul,
There in the fragrant pines and the
    cedars dusk and dim.

1865–6

WHISPERS OF HEAVENLY DEATH

Whispers of heavenly death murmur'd I
    hear,
Labial gossip of night, sibilant chorals,
Footsteps gently ascending, mystical
    breezes wafted soft and low,
Ripples of unseen rivers, tides of a
    current flowing, forever flowing,
(Or is it the plashing of tears? the
    measureless waters of human tears?)

I see, just see skyward, great
    cloud-masses,
Mournfully slowly they roll, silently
    swelling and mixing,
With at times a half-dimm'd sadden'd
    far-off star,
Appearing and disappearing.

(Some parturition rather, some solemn
    immortal birth;
On the frontiers to eyes impenetrable,
Some soul is passing over.)

1868

SO LONG!

To conclude, I announce what comes
    after me.

I remember I said before my leaves
    sprang at all,
I would raise my voice jocund and strong
    with reference to consummations.

When America does what was promis'd,
When through these States walk a
    hundred millions of superb persons,
When the rest part away for superb
    persons and contribute to them,
When breeds of the most perfect mothers
    denote America,
Then to me and mine our due fruition.

I have press'd through in my own right,
I have sung the body and the soul, war
    and peace have I sung, and the songs
    of life and death,
And the songs of birth, and shown that
    there are many births.

I have offer'd my style to every one, I
    have journey'd with confident step;
While my pleasure is yet at the full I
    whisper *So long!*

And take the young woman's hand and
the young man's hand for the last
time.

I announce natural persons
to arise,
I announce justice triumphant,
I announce uncompromising liberty and
equality,
I announce the justification of candor and
the justification of pride.

I announce that the identity of these
States is a single identity only,
I announce the Union more and more
compact, indissoluble,
I announce splendors and majesties to
make all the previous politics of the
earth insignificant.

I announce adhesiveness, I say it shall be
limitless, unloosen'd,
I say you shall yet find the friend you
were looking for.

I announce a man or woman coming,
perhaps you are the one, *(So long!)*
I announce the great individual, fluid as
Nature, chaste, affectionate,
compassionate, fully arm'd.

I announce a life that shall be copious,
    vehement, spiritual, bold,
I announce an end that shall lightly and
    joyfully meet its translation.

I announce myriads of youths, beautiful,
    gigantic, sweet-blooded,
I announce a race of splendid and savage
    old men.

O thicker and faster — *(So long!)*
O crowding too close upon me,
I foresee too much, it means more than I
    thought,
It appears to me I am dying.

Hasten throat and sound your last,
Salute me — salute the days once more.
    Peal the old cry once more.

Screaming electric, the atmosphere
    using,
At random glancing, each as I notice
    absorbing,
Swiftly on, but a little while alighting,
Curious envelop'd messages delivering,
Sparkles hot, seed ethereal down in the
    dirt dropping,
Myself unknowing, my commission
    obeying, to question it never daring,

To ages and ages yet the growth of the
    seed leaving,
To troops out of the war arising, they the
    tasks I have set promulging,
To women certain whispers of myself
    bequeathing, their affection me more
    clearly explaining,
To young men my problems offering —
    no dallier I — I the muscle of their
    brains trying,
So I pass, a little time vocal, visible,
    contrary,

Afterwards a melodious echo, passionately
    bent for, (death making me really
    undying,)
The best of me then when no longer
    visible, for toward that I have been
    incessantly preparing.

What is there more, that I lag and pause
    and crouch extended with unshut
    mouth?
Is there a single final farewell?

My songs cease, I abandon them,
From behind the screen where I hid I
    advance personally solely to you.

Camerado, this is no book,

Who touches this touches a man,
(Is it night? are we here together alone?)
It is I you hold and who holds you,
I spring from the pages into your arms —
    decease calls me forth.

O how your fingers drowse me,
Your breath falls around me like dew,
    your pulse lulls the tympans of my
    ears,
I feel immerged from head to foot,
Delicious, enough.

Enough O deed impromptu and secret,
Enough O gliding present — enough O
    summ'd-up past.

Dear friend whoever you are take this
    kiss,
I give it especially to you, do not forget
    me,
I feel like one who has done work for the
    day to retire awhile,
I receive now again of my many
    translations, from my avataras
    ascending, while others doubtless
    await me,
An unknown sphere more real than I
    dream'd, more direct, darts
    awakening rays about me, *So long!*

260

Remember my words, I may again return,
I love you, I depart from materials,
I am as one disembodied, triumphant,
   dead.

                                    1860